# LUTHER'S
# ENGLISH
# CONNECTION

# LUTHER'S ENGLISH CONNECTION

*The Reformation Thought
Of Robert Barnes and William Tyndale*

## james edward mcgoldrick

Illustrated by Roy Behrens
and K. Dyble Thompson

Northwestern Publishing House
Milwaukee, Wisconsin

*ACKNOWLEDGMENTS*

The following copyright holders kindly granted permission to quote at length from their publications as listed below:

CAMBRIDGE UNIVERSITY PRESS: Chapter **2**, note 39; **3**, 59; from *Studies in the Making of the English Protestant Tradition*, E. G. Rupp; copyright 1966 by Cambridge University Press; reprinted by permission of Cambridge University Press.

CONCORDIA PUBLISHING HOUSE: Chapter **3**, notes 48, 66; **4**, 34, 39; **5**, 66; from *Luther's Works*, Vols. 1, 9, 22, 26, 27; copyright 1957, 1958, 1960, and 1962 by Concordia Publishing House; used by permission of Concordia Publishing House.

FORTRESS PRESS: Chapter **2**, note 63; **3**, 19, 28; **4**, 1, 4, 19, 20, 31, 62; **5**, 27, 31, 45, 60, 75, 88; **6**, 3, 4, 10, 12, 73-75, 84, 87; **7**, 3-8; from *Luther's Works*, Vols. 32, 34-37, 40, 41, 43, 45, 54; copyright 1958-1962, 1966-1968 by Fortress Press; reprinted by permission of Fortress Press.

GREENWOOD PRESS, INC.: Chapter **2**, note 107; **5**, 91; **6**, 66; from *William Tyndale*, by J. F. Mozley, copyright 1971 by Greenwood Press, Inc.: used by permission of the reprint publisher, Greenwood Press, Inc.

HARPER AND ROW PUBLISHERS: Chapter **1**, notes 7, 12; from *Christian Humanism and the Reformation*, John E. Olin, ed.; copyright 1961 by Harper and Row Publishers; reprinted by permission of Harper and Row Publishers.

PRINCETON UNIVERSITY PRESS: Chapter **2**, note 8; from *Tudor Prelates and Politics*, by Lacey Baldwin Smith; copyright 1953 by Princeton University Press; reprinted by permission of Princeton University Press.

YALE UNIVERSITY PRESS: Chapter **2**, note 38; **3**, 66; **5**, 77, 78, 80, 82, 89; **6**, 37; **7**, 22; from *England's Earliest Protestants*, by William A. Clebsch; copyright 1964 by Yale University Press; reprinted by permission of Yale University Press.

# CONTENTS

# PREFACE

Until rather recently almost all writers on the relationship between the English and Continental Reformations assumed that Robert Barnes and William Tyndale were key figures in the transmission of Luther's theology to the British Isles. Most books which dealt with this subject categorically stated that Barnes and Tyndale were Protestant theologians of a basically Lutheran persuasion. In the second half of the 20th century, however, a few scholars have recognized that the traditional view of Barnes and Tyndale had never been adequately documented, and, consequently, they have proposed a reinterpretation which holds that these two reformers, especially Tyndale, were actully Erasmian humanists for whom morality rather than theology was the chief concern. The present writer's study of the sources has led him to the conclusion that the traditional view is completely valid with regard to Barnes, and, with some qualifications, generally correct for Tyndale as well. In the case of the latter, it is evident that he disagreed sharply with Luther on the meaning and importance of the eucharistic presence, and his method of defending infant baptism was quite different from Luther's. Because of the great importance that Luther attached to the Eucharist, and in view of Tyndale's divergence from that view, it is probably not appropriate to identify Tyndale simply as an "English Lutheran," as we may confidently do with Barnes. A careful contextual study of the sources has, nevertheless, convinced this author that Tyndale agreed with Luther in almost every area of doctrine except the Lord's Supper, and that the English reformer very often stated his position in terms which were characteristically Lutheran. It is the purpose of the book to re-examine the traditional interpretation, presenting the evidence for it in a systematic, documented form. The conclusion reached supports the traditional position in general, though with some noteworthy exceptions. Such exceptions notwithstanding, both Barnes and Tyndale were vital links in the chain of Luther's English connection. The controversial interpretive literature is reviewed in chapter 5.

I wish to thank Mr. Howell Heaney and the staff of the Rare Book Department of the Free Library of Philadelphia for allowing me access to most of the original sources on which this study is based. Regrettably, it is now impossible to express appropriate thanks to the one who first suggested this topic. Dr. Carl S. Meyer, Director of the Foundation for Reformation Research, is no longer with us. Of course, thanks are due to my professors in Reformation history, Dr. Elizabeth Hudson and Dr. Mortimer Levine, whose splendid teaching and wise counsel have been a source of great encouragement. The helpful suggestions of Dr. Manfred O. Meitzen and Dr. Ottomar F. Cypris of the Department of Religious Studies at West Virginia University have also been invaluable. Thanks are also due to Dr. Phillip Edgcumbe Hughes of Westminster Theological Seminary who made several suggestions to improve my work, to my son, James E. McGoldrick, Jr., who reviewed the manuscript and to Mrs. Clara Pack who typed it.

Thanks are likewise due to the Rev. John A. Trapp of Northwestern Publishing House who carefully edited this work and made important suggestions to improve it.

James E. McGoldrick
Cedarville, Ohio

## CHAPTER 1

# INTRODUCTION

## THE LEGACY OF LOLLARDY

More than a century before the appearance of Luther's writings in England, the country was convulsed by the vociferous anticlericalism and unorthodox religious teachings of John Wyclif (d. 1384) and the Lollards. Wyclif and his followers assailed long-standing ecclesiastical corruptions such as clerical immorality, simony and the wealth of bishops who neglected their clerical responsibilities. Wyclif likewise advanced a theory of "Civil Dominion," which called on the secular authorities to deprive negligent and corrupt clerics of their properties.

In the realm of doctrine, Wyclif reacted to papal censures of his anticlericalism by assuming theological positions which assaulted the very heart of the medieval church. He was especially alienated from traditional orthodoxy by the scandal of a divided Christendom when rival popes established competing sees at Rome and Avignon in 1378. After this, Wyclif rejected eucharistic transubstantiation and denied that the sacraments were means of saving grace. In Augustinian fashion, he defined the true Church as the body of those predestined for salvation. The pope he branded as Antichrist.

Wyclif justified these radical departures from established dogma by direct appeal to the Bible, which became for him the supreme authority. In 1382, he rendered the authoritative Scriptures into the English language.[1] Theologically and ecclesiologically, Wyclif foreshadowed the reformers of the sixteenth century in so many ways that he has often been hailed as the "Morningstar of the Protestant Reformation."

By the opening of the fifteenth century, the English clergy were able to secure government support in their resistance to heresy, and parliament enacted a law for the arrest and execution of convicted heretics. Persecution decimated the ranks of the Lollards, but adherents to their beliefs were sporadically tried for heresy even into the sixteenth century. The Wyclif translation, as emended by his disciples, remained in circulation long after the Lollards were compelled by persecution to adopt a clandestine existence.[2] Lollard doctrines, such as their denial of transubstantiation and their attacks upon clerical corruption, became pronounced features of Protestant movements of the sixteenth century, and Lollard insistence upon the supreme authority of the Bible foreshadowed the Protestant reformers' demand for *sola scriptura.* Some Protestants reprinted Lollard tracts and books in order to establish historical precedents for their evangelical doctrines,[3] and enemies of the Reformation such as Sir Thomas More were quick to charge the Protestants with perpetuating condemned Wyclifite views.[4]

## THE METHODOLOGY OF HUMANISM

Although the Lollards were the obvious precursors of English Protestantism, the Reformation derived its method of scholarship from Catholic humanism. During the fifteenth century, the magnetic allure of the "new learning" in Italy attracted a number of English scholars to study under Italian masters such as Guarino at Ferrara and Vittorino at Mantua. Apparently, Vittorino's school supplied something of a pattern for the foundations of the English public school system, while the work of Guarino attracted the interest of Humphrey, Duke of Gloucester, a generous patron of humanist manuscriptural scholarship. However, most of Guarino's English students did not make humanist studies a career. They had civil and/or ecclesiastical positions, which were their first concern, and neo-classical studies were almost a hobby with them. Consequently they did not contribute directly to the emergence of a humanist profession in England.

English humanist learning during the fifteenth century was almost a clerical monopoly, and few clerics saw any great distinction between scholasticism and the new approach to study. They saw the humanist method as a tool for the scholastic study of philosophy and theology.[5] It was the sixteenth century before humanism in England achieved independent status as an avenue of scholarship. In this century London became the great humanist center where the merchant and professional classes sought the benefits of the new learning to equip themselves for their duties in the state.

Humanists followed Plato in stressing proper education for those who govern, and they proposed a corresponding curriculum and educational methods. From this point forward, through the reign of Elizabeth I, humanist learning was adapted to the service of the state. This civic complexion of humanism in Tudor times is reflected in the government careers of celebrated scholars such as Thomas More, Thomas Starkey and Thomas Elyot.

Although sixteenth century English humanism was civic in orientation, it was by no means exclusively secular. Humanist-clerics also pursued the new learning in the interest of making it an instrument for ecclesiastical reform. The humanist efforts in this direction were initiated by distinguished scholars such as John Colet, who studied first at Oxford and later in Italy. Colet became a close friend of Erasmus, who made five visits to England, beginning in 1499. Some hold that Colet's influence led Erasmus into the study of the Bible and Christian foundations.[6] Both of these scholars were openly critical of clerical corruptions. Speaking of Colet, Erasmus observed:

> There was no class of persons to whom he was more opposed or for whom he had greater abhorrence than those bishops who acted the part of wolves instead of shepherds, showing themselves off before the people with their guise of sanctity, their ceremonies, benedictions, and paltry indulgences, while at heart they were slaves to the world, that is, to ostentation and gain.[7]

When Colet became Dean of St. Paul's Cathedral during the reign of Henry VII, he adopted the humanist method of Biblical exposition in his preaching. He departed from the customary liturgical practice of building homilies on isolated texts and concentrated instead on expounding entire books of the Bible or connected doctrinal themes such as in the Apostles' Creed.[8]

Dean Colet employed the grammatical-exegetical method, which would be adopted by the major Protestant reformers, and the doctrinal conclusions which he reached were remarkably similar to theirs in certain important points. He shared their Augustinian convictions regarding human depravity and predestination, and there is some evidence that he was inclined toward a view of justification compatible with the later Protestant position.[9]

While at Oxford, Colet urged students to study the Scriptures, and a group of earnest Bible students did develop Magdalen College, of which William Tyndale became a member.[10] Although Tyndale may not have known Colet personally, it seems certain the legacy of Colet's influence was strong at Oxford even after he departed for London to become Dean of St. Paul's.

Evidently, Lollard doctrine and humanist methodology converged to a degree in Colet even before they appeared in Protestant reformers such as Robert Barnes and William

ABOVE: Erasmus of Rotterdam    BELOW: the church at Aldington in Kent, England, where Erasmus served as rector in 1511, while he was also delivering lectures at Cambridge.

Tyndale. Colet's preaching excited enthusiasm among Lollards who seemed to regard him as a kindred spirit.[11]

Furthermore, the Lollard and Protestant demand for Scripture in the vernacular also had parallels among the humanists. In the preface to his 1516 Greek and Latin edition of the New Testament, Erasmus registered his desire to see the Scriptures published in the common tongue:

> Would that . . . the farmer sing some portion of them at the plow, the weaver hum some parts of them to the movement of his shuttle, the traveller lighten the weariness of the journey with stories of this kind! Let all the conversations of every Christian be drawn from this source.[12]

Although Erasmus did not personally produce a vernacular translation of the Bible, his Greek-Latin New Testament inspired others to do so. Martin Luther used it as the basis for the New Testament portion of his *Deutsche Bibel,* and Tyndale employed it in his rendering of the New Testament into English. The appearance of Erasmus' New Testament at Cambridge had a quick and heavy impact upon men who were to become the pioneers of the English Reformation. Among them was the Austin prior Robert Barnes.

So it appears that there is a two-fold background against which the thought of the English Protestant reformers should be studied. The first portion is the doctrinal legacy from Wyclif, with whom both Barnes and Tyndale had much in common, and the second is the scholarly methodology of humanism, which both of these reformers broadly and effectively used.

# THE BIOGRAPHICAL BACKGROUND

## ROBERT BARNES (1495-1540)

*Reformer-Churchman*

Robert Barnes was born at Lynn in Norfolk, about 40 miles from Cambridge where he enrolled with the Austin friars in 1514. He must have been a promising student, for in 1517 he was sent for advanced study at the University of Louvain, which had become a leading center of humanist scholarship. Exactly how long Barnes remained there is not known, but it is known that Erasmus was at Louvain from 1517-21; so it is probable that the two men met. However, no documentary evidence has yet been discovered to suggest any close association between them.

Upon his return from Louvain, as a Doctor of Divinity, Barnes showed that he had imbibed the spirit and methodology of humanism. This became evident after he was made Austin prior at Cambridge, in which position he promoted educational reforms in the Erasmian style. His zeal for such reforms earned him recognition as the "restorer of letters."[1]

From the martyrologist John Foxe we learn that Barnes introduced the Austin friars to the study of such classical authors as Terence, Plautus and Cicero. Barnes also brought with him from Louvain one Thomas Parnell, an energetic disciple of the new learning, who assisted him in implementing humanist reforms. The result — Barnes "caused the house shortly to flourish with good letters, and made a great part of the house learned (who before were drowned in barbarous rudeness)."[2]

The introduction of classical authors was soon followed by the study of the Pauline Epistles of the New Testament. Apparently, this was the launching-pad for Barnes' projectiles of criticism against the religious establishment. As Foxe reports it, he became "mighty in the Scriptures, preaching ever against bishops and hypocrites."[3] This evidently means that Barnes had become a crusader against ecclesiastical abuses but had not yet embraced Protestant doctrine. In fact, Foxe states quite emphatically that strong preaching on moral themes preceded Barnes' discussions with Master Thomas Bilney who "converted him wholly unto Christ."[4] Bilney was a Cambridge scholar who also denounced clerical corruptions. However, he went beyond humanist demands by espousing Protestant theological principles.

Bilney was one of the first Cambridge reformers to accept actual Evangelical theological views. He helped to start a movement that would earn for his university the reputation of being England's incubator of heretics.[5]

In addition to leading Barnes into the Evangelical camp, Bilney persuaded Hugh Latimer to adhere to the same cause. He did so in a most intriguing way. Since Latimer was a priest, Bilney asked him to hear his confession, and while on his knees in the posture of a penitent, Bilney unfolded the Evangelical message to his confessor! This is quite remarkable in light of the fact that Latimer had already taken a public stand against Protestant beliefs in his oration for the Bachelor of Divinity where he had lashed out against Philip Melanchthon, Luther's principal co-worker at Wittenberg.[6] Bilney's personal conversion to Evangelical views seems to have taken place as a result of reading the

New Testament of Erasmus and some treatises of Martin Luther. Foxe may have exaggerated Bilney's influence by suggesting that it carried Barnes completely into the Protestant faith, but it is certain that Bilney at least introduced him to Evangelical doctrines. And Bilney's influence with Latimer clearly was decisive.

Thomas Bilney also has been credited with founding a study group of Cambridge men interested in the discussion of reformist ideas and, perhaps, even some "Lutheran" concepts. With Bilney, Barnes and Latimer as a nucleus, the group met at the White Horse Inn as early as 1518, when Luther's writings had not yet been proscribed. Because of their rumored interest in Lutheran doctrines, the tavern was nicknamed "Little Germany," and the group that met there the "Cambridge Germans."

> The White Horse tavern was at the time a place of no importance in the sight of the University or the State. It was just the place where the young aired their extreme views and proposed reforms which their reverend seniors were certain could not be carried through.[7]

Nevertheless, the White Horse meetings attracted men who were destined to be remembered as key figures in England's travails during the era of the struggle for reform. Some of them eventually became Anglican bishops. "Among their group were enthusiastic critics of church, state, and university alike, youthful humanists, and indiscreet students who enjoyed the chance to express personal opinions without regard to authority."[8] Barnes gradually became the leader at White Horse but not in any official capacity. At the end of 1520, Luther's writings were banned, and it may be that after that date the meetings at White Horse assumed a clandestine character.

Because Bilney, Barnes, and Latimer, in their early preachings, attacked clerical abuses and superstitions, they incurred the scornful opposition of clerics who felt personally affronted. They had not yet, however, publicly preached

ABOVE: Robert Barnes and Cambridge's White Horse Inn, the "birthplace of the English Reformation" BELOW: citizens of 16th-Century Europe (from an engraving by Albrecht Duerer)

anything which would be indisputably heretical. Apparently, Robert Barnes was the first of the White Horse men to cross the line which separated tolerable criticism from heretical pronouncements. When he crossed that line, Barnes became perhaps "the most troublesome heretic of that time."[9]

Although Barnes was utterly tactless in denouncing abuses wherever he found them, his criticisms of noteworthy clerics did not make him liable to prosecution for heresy. But Barnes was not content to stop there. With reckless disregard for his own security, on Christmas Sunday, 1525, Dr. Barnes preached at St. Edward's Church, Cambridge, a pulpit from which Latimer had already been excluded. Barnes took to the pulpit with a sermon which denounced the material wealth and splendor of the clergy when compared with the poverty of Christ at his nativity. But the feature of the sermon which aroused the charge of heresy was Barnes' declaration that a Christian could not legitimately sue a fellow Christian at the civil magistracy. This brought the accusation that Barnes was advocating subversive Anabaptist tenets.[10]

Barnes' remarks were very untimely because this was the period of the Peasants' Revolt in Germany. So England's civil and religious establishment was understandably alarmed at a sermon thought to contain revolutionary implications.

The incident provoked by the Christmas sermon well illustrates Barnes' characteristic indifference to his own safety. Because he was the Austin prior, he could operate freely within his own monastic house without much fear of reprisal from Cambridge University. The Austins at Cambridge did not receive financial subsidies from the crown as some other orders did, so they enjoyed more freedom to initiate educational reforms. Consequently, the pulpit of the priory "more than once served as a sounding board for reform-minded sermons."[11]

As a consequence of his recklessness, Barnes was summoned before Cardinal Wolsey, in whose presence he conducted himself indiscreetly, to say the least. The Christmas sermon had contained unflattering references to Wolsey, which the Lord Chancellor probably interpreted as a personal insult. Wolsey complained: "We were jollily that day laughed to scorn. Verily it was a sermon more fit to be preached on a stage than in a pulpit."[12]

Although Wolsey surely felt affronted by Barnes' pointed criticisms of clerical wealth and pomp, the Cardinal was probably even more alarmed over the social implications of the sermon. Nevertheless, despite his lack of penitence and humility at the hearing, Barnes did not fare too badly. His cause was aided by influential friends and vociferous sympathizers. Prior to his appearance before Cardinal Wolsey, Barnes had been given two preliminary hearings before lesser officials. Both hearings had to be disbanded because of the strength of the student reaction. The students rallied in support of Barnes.[13]

At the hearing before Cardinal Wolsey, Barnes was fortunate in having the advocacy of Stephen Gardiner, secretary to the Cardinal, and of Edward Fox, Master of Wards. They appealed to Wolsey: "We desire your grace to be good unto him, for he will be reformable."[14] Barnes then asked for and was given a formal trial where he supported his position by copiously citing the Scriptures and Church Fathers. Even though his life was in danger, he resisted the pleas of his friends to recant.

The importance of the trial extended well beyond its significance for Barnes personally. Evidently, some meaning should be attached to the speed with which the authorities brought his case to court. It may suggest that Barnes' offense went beyond the declarations of his Christmas sermon. In addition to the haste in arranging a trial, it should be noted that the commission which investigated Barnes was the same one which Wolsey had earlier formed to investigate those suspected of circulating heretical literature. Barnes was accused at the very time that Wolsey was pressing for the seizure and destruction of "Lutheran" books.

There is reason to believe that Barnes was suspected of having a part in the dissemination of alien religious writings. Tyndale's edition of the New Testament was rolling off the presses in Cologne at this time. Barnes must have known about it, for a short time later, while under house arrest, he was found to be engaged in selling New Testaments of that edition.[15]

In his predicament, Barnes began to yield to the pressures of his friends, and he agreed to recant. He was then assigned a public penance at Paul's Cross in London where he was to walk in a procession and carry a fagot lighted for all to see — a symbol of that punishment which was reserved for heretics. As one interpreter sees it, this was timed to coincide with the trial and public penance of some Steelyard merchants from Germany who were accused of being agents for the importation of Lutheran books.[16] The residences at Cambridge had been searched, but no heretical literature had been found there. Nevertheless, a book-burning was held for those objectionable works which were on hand, and the Steelyard merchants and Dr. Barnes did public penance together. "The injection of Prior Barnes was just what was needed to give a fillip to what otherwise might have been a flat performance."[17]

This is a plausible explanation, for a letter dated 5 January 1526 reveals that Wolsey had been campaigning strongly against "Lutheran" literature. The Cardinal wrote to the Bishop of Lincoln arranging a book-burning at which John Fisher, a noted enemy of the Evangelicals, was to preach against Luther.[18]

Because he recanted, Barnes' life was spared. But he was still incarcerated in the Fleet Prison, where he was to remain "till the Lord Cardinal's pleasure was known."[19] After six months, he was placed under house arrest at the priory of his order in London. There he again abandoned all caution by selling Tyndale New Testaments to some Lollards. When word of this reached the authorities, Barnes was removed to the "Austin Friars of Northampton, there to be burned."[20]

But late in 1529 Barnes escaped the stake by a clever and elaborate ruse, which sent his pursuers dragging the river for his body after they had read his "suicide" note. He next appeared in Antwerp, and from there he went to Germany. Once he was safe, Barnes assailed Gardiner for leading him to deny the truth, though Gardiner had helped to save his life.[21] Eventually, Barnes arrived in Wittenberg where he became a close friend of Luther and Melanchthon. There, in the heartland of the Reformation, his transition to Lutheranism was completed.

While in Wittenberg, Robert Barnes began writing his *Vitae Romanorum Pontificum,* a work which is noteworthy because it was the first Protestant history of the papacy,[22] and because it shows that its author had adopted a consistently Evangelical theology.[23] Barnes' first controversial sermon had been composed along the lines of Luther's postil for that day; now he was with Luther in Germany, using his pen to promote the reform of the English Church along the theological lines of Lutheranism.

By the time Barnes had fled to Germany, the doctrinal complexion of the "Cambridge Germans" had become definitely Protestant. Those reformers had once been mostly Erasmians, but, by 1530, they "parted company with Erasmus where Erasmus had parted company with Luther."[24] Actually, the Cambridge group split into mutually exclusive factions over the controversy on the role of the human will in salvation, which saw Erasmus and Luther exchange opposing treatises in 1524-25. Those who accepted Luther's view in *De Servo Arbitrio* went on to become the champions of a Protestant Reformation for England, whereas those who sided with Erasmus mostly remained with the Church of Rome.[25]

There is no doubt whatever that Robert Barnes was the most thoroughly Lutheran reformer of the White Horse group. His theology was firmly and fully developed by 1530, and whereas the term "Lutheran" was carelessly and inaccurately attached to almost anyone with Evangelical leanings, it was literally correct when applied to Dr. Barnes. His theological writings reflect the pronounced influence of Luther, and at times it appears that Barnes deliberately paraphrased his German mentor. This will become more apparent in our discussion of Barnes' views on the controverted doctrinal issues of the Reformation era.

The bombastic and forceful apologetical approach of Robert Barnes is reminiscent of Luther's style. Stephen Gardiner had once described Barnes as "a trymme minion frere Augustine, one of merye skoffynge witte, frerelike, and as a good fellowe in company was beloved by many."[26] Gardiner, however, did not long maintain this affectionate view, for the now intractable Lutheran theologian could no longer be excused as an impetuous humanist reformer. Barnes had become a Lutheran in temperament as well as theology, at one point denouncing his doctrinal opponents as "crooked enemies of Christ's blood."[27]

This avowed Lutheranism, so aggressively stated, made Robert Barnes *persona non grata* in an England where the royal "Defender of the Faith" was seeking to maintain his personal interpretation of Catholicism in opposition to the reformers. "The king realized that by taking active measures against heretical books he could demonstrate his unwavering orthodoxy and relieve the anxieties of conservatives."[28]

At the risk of continuing to aggravate his king, Dr. Barnes used his pen to play the role of reformer-in-exile. All of his theological writings, the vast majority of them in the vernacular, eventually appeared in England where they were used to good effect by the apostles of Protestantism.

## Reformer-Diplomat

One of the remarkable aspects of Barnes' career is the fact that he invariably made an impression wherever he went. He rarely suffered from being ignored, either by friend or foe. In Germany he quickly gained admission to the inner circle of religious and political leaders. As Foxe summarizes:

> In the mean season Dr. Barnes was made strong in Christ, and got favor both with the learned in Christ, and with foreign princes in Germany, and was great with Luther, Melanchthon, Pomeran, Justus Jonas, Hegendorphinus, and Aepinus, and with the Duke of Saxony, and with the King of Denmark.[29]

The good impression that his subject made on the Continent did not long go unnoticed by Henry VIII and his advisers. Almost as soon as the Smalkald League was formed as a defensive alliance of Protestant princes (1531), England was invited to join. Henry was interested for two reasons. He was seeking support for his divorce from Catherine of Aragon, which the pope had refused to allow, and he felt the need for allies against France and/or Spain.

By the end of 1530, Pope Clement VII, under pressure from Emperor Charles V, was becoming increasingly difficult in his dealings with Henry. The pope declared that the king could not cohabit with any woman other than Catherine and prohibited anyone, including university faculties and civil courts, from passing judgment on Henry's case. This exasperated Henry and drove him to seek support wherever he could find it, even from the Lutherans for whom he earlier had nothing but scorn.[30]

During 1530, Henry may have spent as much as 5000 crowns in soliciting German opinions on the divorce question.[31] In 1531, William Paget arrived in Germany as Henry's envoy to initiate discussions relative to the king's matrimonial troubles. This was the first of a series of contacts which brought Barnes back to England, where he was then commissioned as the royal ambassador to represent his king's interests to the Lutherans. The summons into the royal service came to Barnes in the same year that he composed the first edition of his *Supplication unto King Henry the Eighth*. Much in the same manner that his fellow Protestant exile, William Tyndale, had written *The Obedience of a Christian Man*, Barnes wrote to protest his steadfast loyalty to the monarch. Moreover, Barnes endorsed the concept of royal supremacy in ecclesiastical affairs, while he attacked the English bishops as enemies of the king's lawful authority.

The *Supplication* was received in England by Thomas Cromwell, Henry's chief minister, from Stephen Vaughan, who was Cromwell's commercial agent in Antwerp. Vaughan wrote to his employer on 14 November 1531, saying, "I beg you will deliver Barnes' book to the King in his name."[32] A copy of Tyndale's exposition of the Epistle of 1 John was sent at the same time. In his letter, Vaughan seemed to be trying to impress the king with his own diligence and loyalty in the royal service. Concerning Barnes' book, Vaughan urged Cromwell: "look well upon Dr. Barnes' book. I think he shall seal it with his blood."[33] Nevertheless, by late December, Barnes was back in England under a promise of safe conduct from the king himself.[34] For the next nine years, Barnes would be engaged in the king's service. As it has aptly been observed, Henry was the self-appointed preserver of traditional doctrine, but "while disavowing heresy openly, and even persecuting it, he was glad to avail himself of the aid of heretics . . . in the special business of overthrowing the Pope's authority."[35]

Henry brought Barnes back to England because he thought he could be useful. But Barnes' career in the royal service had an unfortunate beginning. Barnes brought with him Luther's reply to the king's divorce inquiry. Luther denied the validity of Henry's case. The king's rejection of Luther's remarks must have injured Barnes' standing too, for "Henry was not the kind of man who would look benignly on the bearer of bad tidings."[36]

Despite this unfortunate beginning, a year later Robert Barnes was made a royal chaplain. Still, this did not mean that Barnes was totally secure in the king's favor. Barnes and all Protestant reformers had one implacable enemy in high places, and that was Lord Chancellor Thomas More, successor to Cardinal Wolsey, who had fallen from the good graces of the king in 1529. In More's estimation Barnes was an incorrigible heretic and should be dealt with accordingly. Just as Cromwell showed sympathy for the Protestant exiles and sent agents to encourage them to return home, so More's agents hounded them as heretics.[37] More "argued that the Church taught truth, the Protestants opposed the Church, *ergo* the Protestants taught lies."[38] More's agents dogged Barnes' steps in England, and More himself wrote:

> Barnes but for the King's safe conduct he should have standed in peril to be burned and his books with him which safe conduct because it was granted but for six weeks now more than almost passed.[39]

For once, Dr. Barnes was able to interpret the course of events and the climate of the times in his own interest. He knew that the hostility of More made it unsafe to remain in England, so he left for Germany. However, at this point, Henry did not share his chancellor's intractable hatred for Barnes, for even after his return to Germany, Barnes' *Supplication* continued to be printed in England with royal consent.[40] The departure from England did not mark the end of Barnes' role as a royal diplomatic servant. If anything, just the reverse was true. Until his death in 1540, Barnes was intermittently employed as Henry's man on the Continent.

The year 1532 found Robert Barnes in Hamburg where he served as assistant pastor in a Lutheran parish for several months. By mid-1533, he was again in Wittenberg, enrolled at the university and completing the writing of his *Vitae Romanorum Pontificum,* which would be published in 1535. Meanwhile, from 1532-36, Henry continued making rather irregular overtures to the Lutheran princes. After the failure of Barnes to bring a favorable response from Luther on the divorce question, however, the king's objective with the Lutherans was more political than theological or matrimonial. He was primarily seeking England's membership in the Smalkald League as a means to prevent his country from being diplomatically isolated. When other avenues toward that goal appeared, Henry cooled toward the League.[41]

Dr. Barnes again became involved in Henry's diplomatic efforts in 1533. The king had approached John Frederick, Elector of Saxony, with an offer of alliance but was rebuffed because the prince feared that such a combination would provoke Emperor Charles. From Henry's perspective, however, the picture soon appeared to brighten considerably. Luebeck, the dominant city of the Hanseatic League, was now Lutheran, and Jurgen Wullenwever, the burgomaster, was leading the city in a bold policy designed to obtain control of the Baltic. The burgomaster boasted that no one would sit upon the vacant throne of Denmark without Luebeck's approval. Moreover, he approached Henry with the suggestion that the King of England might be a candidate acceptable to Luebeck. The crown appeared to be a tempting prize, so Henry was interested and chose Robert Barnes to represent his interests in northern Europe.[42] A diplomatic mission from the Hanseatic League, but representing only Luebeck and Hamburg, arrived in England in June 1534, and there was division of opinion among its members. Meanwhile, Charles V was trying to influence the Danish Estates to choose the Elector Palatine as their king. Henry then encouraged the Hanse in the choice of a Lutheran king in order to outflank Charles in the north. Christian III was elected; he was a Lutheran, but not the candidate approved by Luebeck. Thereafter, fighting broke out between the forces of the new Danish king and those of Luebeck. Henry supported Luebeck, but he was backing a lost cause. Barnes, who realized this, tried, to no avail, to warn him. Luebeck was defeated, and Henry lost his chance to establish an alliance which could have restricted Charles V in northern Germany and Scandanavia.

Had his sovereign accepted Barnes' advice to seek an alliance with the new Danish king, Henry's fortunes in northern Europe might have been considerably better. By August 1534 Dr. Barnes had returned to England. But early in 1535 this "trouble shooter" was once again on his way to the Continent to serve the interests of the king to whom he was always most loyal. This time the mission was to thwart French King Francis I, who was looking for leverage against Charles V.

Specifically, Francis had invited Philip Melanchthon of the University of Wittenberg to visit Paris. Francis wanted Melanchthon to draw the optimistic conclusion that he might be receptive to the Evangelical faith. In this way, King Francis was playing Henry's game of religious and diplomatic duplicity. Barnes was ordered to use his influence with the Lutherans to foil Francis by inviting Melanchthon to England. His goal was to convince the Germans that Henry was sincerely interested in the Protestant Reform and that he was ready to join the League.[43] Henry evidently feared that a Franco-Lutheran agreement might destroy his own opportunity for such an alliance.

The Elector of Saxony refused to allow Melanchthon to go to either Paris or London, and by 1535 Luther was personally convinced that Henry VIII would never be won for the Reformation. Nevertheless, some of the Lutheran princes still wanted to pursue the possibility of an alignment with England, as they did not share Luther's pessimism about

Henry's potential for conversion to Protestant views. Since Barnes was hailed throughout the Evangelical states, he was still the ideal public relations man for the king's cause in Germany. Thomas Cromwell was still striving for an Anglo-German alliance, and an English delegation, composed of Nicholas Heath — Archdeacon of Stafford, Edward Fox — Bishop of Hereford, and Barnes, opened discussions in Smalkald at Christmas time in 1535. Although Barnes himself finally admitted that he did not think his king to be genuinely interested in religion, he still pushed for an agreement which would make Anglo-German diplomatic collaboration possible. The nature of these discussions, however, was to explore the possibility of doctrinal concord as a preliminary to any political agreement.[44]

Although the Lutheran princes were willing to have Henry as a partner in the Smalkald League, they made membership contingent upon Henry's adherence to the *Augsburg Confession*. The king's reply to this proposal was a polite refusal to commit himself so precisely on doctrine. He never seemed to realize that civil rulers could take religious issues so seriously that they would permit them to preclude political decisions. Because of their king's lack of appreciation for the theological matters involved, his negotiators could not achieve any agreement on his behalf. Henry clearly felt himself superior to his German counterparts and regarded their demand for doctrinal conformity as conduct unbecoming mere princes who were addressing themselves to a king. "The King knowing himself to be the learnedest prince in Europe, he thought it became him not to submit to them; but he expected they should submit to him."[45]

The theological discussions at Smalkald finally produced a statement of faith in the form of the *Wittenberg Articles*, compiled mainly by Philip Melanchthon. In this document the Lutherans set forth their doctrinal requirements. Henry replied with a statement of his own — the *Ten Articles*, which evaded the real issues. The doctrinal impasse at this time, however, did not stop attempts to reach an agreement. In fact, such attempts continued sporadically until 1540.

> For almost fifteen years Henry carried on a doctrinal dance with the German Protestants, a religious minuet in which both parties bowed and swayed to the theological melody of Wittenberg but rarely touched hands, let alone danced cheek-to-cheek.[46]

Although the Smalkald negotiations do not mark any significant change in Anglo-German relations, they do indicate when the personal standing of Robert Barnes with his monarch had begun to decline. In 1535, Barnes had been in such favor with Henry that a Roman priest was indicted for offenses against the crown, including the charge that he had insulted Barnes by calling him a "false fellow and a naughty wretch . . . that it was a great shame to suffer him to preach anywhere."[47] At Smalkald, on the other hand, the English negotiating team was led by Bishop Edward Fox, who did not share Barnes' enthusiasm for Lutheranism. Henry did not intend to allow Barnes to sway the delegation toward accepting a really Protestant position. Little did the king realize that one day Fox would join the ranks of England's Protestant reformers.

After the failure of Barnes to obtain a favorable opinion from Luther on the divorce question, Henry's overtures to the Lutherans were mainly political. This is not to suggest, however, that he ceased to be interested in getting a Lutheran endorsement of his divorce, if that were possible. Until Catherine died in January 1536, efforts were made in that direction, and in those efforts Barnes played a conspicuous role. Luther and his fellow theologians in Germany were firm in their refusal to endorse the king's position, even when to do so could have brought political advantages to the Protestant cause. Barnes was not the cause of his own political failure. He was a faithful royal servant who persistently used his influence on Henry's behalf, but even his "inside track" with the reformers did not obtain a favorable verdict for his king. After the death of Catherine, however, it no longer mattered, and Henry's concern with the Germans became entirely political.

The year 1535 marks something of a peak so far as the personal fortunes of Robert Barnes are concerned. This is confirmed by an interesting piece of evidence. In May of that year, Henry appointed Barnes to a commission which had been organized to investigate charges of Anabaptism against twenty-three immigrants from Flanders, who were brought to trial at St. Paul's.[48] A little later in the same year, he served on a similar investigating commission with Archbishop Cranmer. Seemingly, the "heretic" had been completely rehabilitated. This, however, merely reflects the whim of the king at a moment when he felt it was to his advantage to keep Barnes at liberty for his present and future usefulness to the crown. As it has been incisively observed:

> Henry was a complete egotist. If he wished that England should be rich and powerful it was because it was his realm; and if he wished that the Church of England should be a model to Christendom it was because it was his realm.[49]

Robert Barnes was personally satisfied that he had done his work well in connection with the Smalkald discussions and in preventing the visit of Melanchthon to Francis I, so it must have been a disappointment when he learned that Bishop Fox was to be the principal spokesman for the English delegation at those conferences. Whether or not he was able to interpret this as a sign of his declining stand in the eyes of his king cannot be definitely asserted. It is certain, however, that the discussions which began at Smalkald in December 1535 ended at Wittenberg in April 1536 without agreement. And Henry VIII did not look kindly upon those who failed him.

Once back in England, Barnes realized that the atmosphere was becoming unpleasant. By June 1536, he was so fearful that he wrote to Melanchthon warning him not to come to England.[50] Anne Boleyn had recently been executed, and, since she had given some support to the reformers, Barnes and others of his religious persuasion must have felt insecure.[51]

By mid-1536 Dr. Barnes was also in difficult financial straits. Although he had served his king with unswerving loyalty, he had never been suitably rewarded in a material way. The best he could ever get was a remote prebend in Wales worth only eighteen pounds per year.[52] In addition, he was excluded from his monastic order and forbidden to preach. He derived little personal benefit from all that he had done so loyally. At best, the future appeared unpromising. Appearances suggested that "Henry greatly disliked him and that Cromwell durst not advance one whom the King delighted not to honour."[53]

Robert Barnes might have been forsaken as far as royal favor and gratitude were concerned, but he was not forgotten. With the international situation subject to change at any time, the king knew all too well that this loyal "heretic" might still be of use. By mid-1537, Charles V and Francis I had come to terms, so Henry VIII and the German Lutheran princes again felt the need for each other. Therefore Barnes was once more allowed to preach, and true to form, he began advocating reformist ideas such as conducting worship services in the vernacular tongue.

Early in 1538, Henry resumed serious overtures to the Smalkald League, so Barnes was thrust into the diplomatic arena again. A German mission arrived in England in the spring to discuss a possible alliance based upon doctrinal agreement by mutual subscription to the *Wittenberg Articles*. The discussions dragged on fruitlessly until the next fall, when the Germans, disgusted with Henry's procrastinations, left England. Barnes had striven to achieve theological unity within a Lutheran framework. He failed again, and Anglo-German relations languished.[54]

Each time that the international scene dictated the need for a diplomat with connections in Germany, Barnes was pressed into service, and, despite the lack of recognition and reward which he endured, each time Barnes responded to the royal summons willingly. It seems that Henry would never give Barnes very much, and the little which he did give was awarded only when the king was cultivating him for some future mission. For example, in August 1538 Archbishop Cranmer petitioned the king to appoint Robert Barnes to the deanery of Tamworth College, Staffordshire, which had an annual income of twenty pounds. In October of the same year, he was appointed to a commission to examine heretics. Specifically, the commissioners were to "search for and examine Anabaptists, receive back into the Church such as renounce their error, hand over those who persist in it to the secular arm for punishment, and destroy all books of that detestable sect."[55]

As 1538 drew to a close, Henry found himself again threatened by the monarchs of France and Spain, and there was trouble in Scotland. It was again time to call on Robert Barnes. He was sent on his last diplomatic mission, and "the aim was a political alliance without the bothersome overtones of doctrinal agreement."[56] Barnes called on the rulers in Hamburg and Denmark, but the Lutheran position was unchanged — no political alliance without prior theological accord. The only German state which expressed some interest in an alliance was Cleves — where the Duke was not a Protestant himself, but where the Evangelical faith had made gains within the ruling family.[57]

The Duchy of Cleves seemed to be of strategic value in the European distribution of power. Its lands lay between the Netherlands and Germany, which meant that they blocked the path of Charles V if he should want to move against the Lutheran princes. Cromwell interpreted this as an opportunity for England to acquire leverage by means of a marriage-alliance for Henry with Anne, sister of the Duke. The details of the marriage and subsequent divorce are interesting, but only incidental to our investigation of Barnes' role in the affair.

John Foxe suggests that Barnes was the central figure in arranging the marriage. He says Barnes was "sent ambassador by King Henry VIII to the Duke of Cleves, for the marriage of the lady Anne of Cleves between the king and her."[58] On the basis of this assertion, some have concluded that the direct cause of Barnes' final fall from the royal favor was his role in arranging a marriage which Henry detested from the start. This cannot be substantiated. In fact, there is no collateral evidence to connect Barnes with the affair, and those who did conclude the agreement did not suffer for their mistake.[59]

Since there is no documentary evidence on which to verify Foxe's remarks about Barnes and the royal marriage, we may conclude that the mission to Germany was the last phase of Barnes' diplomatic life. In the early stages of his contacts in Germany there was some reason for encouragement, but it was his own king who made the task impossible by promulgating a sweeping anti-Protestant law at the very time that Barnes was advertising Henry as the savior of Protestantism! The law in question is the *Act of the Six Articles,* passed on 5 May 1539.

Basically, the *Six Articles* were a ringing reaffirmation of Catholic theology. They upheld transubstantiation, clerical celibacy, communion in one kind, private masses, vows of chastity and auricular confession. The death penalty was prescribed for most offenses of unbelief.[60] Once more, Henry's motive in this dramatic move was coldly political. In January 1539 Charles V and Francis I had concluded the Treaty of Toledo. At first this was viewed as a threat to England, but soon the two rulers let it be known that they had no desire to enter a conflict with Henry VIII. Therefore,

> Henry, desiring at once to disarm domestic discontent and to remove all pretext for French or Imperial hostility by convincing Catholic Europe of his entire orthodoxy, urged Parliament . . . to take such action as would banish all diversity of religious opinion from the realm.[61]

This legislation totally deprived Barnes of all chance for success. Continental Protestant reaction was predictably vehement. Casper Cruciger, a professor at Wittenberg, wrote about the matter to Frederick Myconius, a noted Lutheran pastor.

> Philippus [Melanchthon] has written to me that a decree [is] made in England for the retention of the old abuses; it is a capital [crime] to refuse to

dissolve matrimony contracted in violation of
vows. Alesius has escaped and is now at Wittenberg. Antonius* Barnes is at Hamburg and dare
not return to the realm, although he is the King's
ambassador. Many good men are in danger.[62]

Luther's reflections on the alliance negotiations were recorded by his table guest, Anthony Lauterbach.

There's no doubt at all that the king was hindered
by divine intervention because he had always
been unstable. I'm glad that we're rid of the blas-
phemer. He wants to be head of the church in England directly after Christ, a title that isn't appropriate for any bishop or prelate, to say nothing of a
king. It won't do. . . . The devil rides the king who
troubles the church and torments Christ. . . . He's
still King Harry, but he'll soon be confounded.[63]

Protestant reaction to the *Six Articles* seemed to be of
very little concern to King Henry. By this time, he had "little liking for the German alliance, less for his German wife,
and none for German theology"[64] Even if, as it has been suggested, the *Six Articles* were "above all else a panic-mea-
sure, . . . a sudden display of orthodoxy to disarm enemies at
home and abroad,"[65] this was small comfort for Robert
Barnes, who had labored so long for the very agreement
which his royal master now made impossible.

## Reformer-Martyr

In the foreign service of Henry VIII, Robert Barnes
showed himself to be an efficient, though not always suc-

---

*Editor's note: In the 1533 Wittenberg University matriculation records
Robert Barnes is entered as "D. [octor] Antonius Anglus." Luther also
addressed him as "My Antonius" in his correspondence of 3 September
1531.

cessful, diplomat. However, his keen perception in foreign affairs was not matched by a penetrating insight into the significance of changing domestic conditions. His lack of perception here brought injury to his position and, finally, death to his person. Despite reports that a hostile situation had developed in England subsequent to the promulgation of the *Six Articles,* Barnes decided to return home in August 1539. Why he took this risky step is rather difficult to understand, but it may have been because:

> There was always a measure of egotism in Barnes which could not be concealed; he was theatrical, full of bombast, always ready to play up to the crowd. He had all the impulsive excitement which throws discretion overboard, and memory was seldom to prevent him from making the same mistake again.[66]

Whatever his reason for returning, Barnes was an unwelcome ex-ambassador at the royal court. The king did not even grant him the courtesy of an audience to make his official report. Then, to make matters worse, Thomas Cromwell decided that the time was long overdue to give Barnes some tangible reward for his services. Cromwell recommended that he be awarded the prebendry at Lambedye. Since Henry was completely disenchanted with the idea of marriage to Anne of Cleves and blamed Cromwell for the whole affair, the suggestion of rewarding Barnes was badly timed and came from the wrong source. Cromwell and Barnes were now regarded as inseparable in the royal eyes, so the fall of the one was bound to involve the fall of the other. Neither Barnes nor Cromwell seemed to know what was good for them. Even after Henry revealed his displeasure with

Barnes, Cromwell continued to favor him, and so their association would ultimately prove fatal to both.[67]

If Barnes expected to survive in the hostile atmosphere which developed in 1539, reason would seem to dictate that he make himself as inconspicuous as possible. This is precisely what he did not do. True to his primary vocation as a reformer, Barnes began preaching Protestant doctrines almost as soon as he returned from Germany. He did so with the full knowledge that conservative Henrician churchmen would use their influence with the king to his detriment. Stephen Gardiner, Barnes' former friend and protector, had already publicly asked the king to silence Barnes. The tenor of Gardiner's request showed the strength of his resolve to deny Barnes the pulpit as a rostrum from which to promote his Protestant principles. Gardiner besought the king:

> May it please your Majesty, if you allow Dr. Barnes to preach much, all the nation will be lost, and the people will become such heretics that they will not recognize either God or your Majesty.[68]

At first, Henry did not move against Barnes for his offensive preaching of heresy, so Barnes may have thought that he would not be molested. In February 1540, Heinrich Bullinger, the successor to Zwingli in Zurich, received a letter from England which stated, "the Word is powerfully preached by one Barnes and his fellow ministers. Books of every kind may be safely exposed to sale."[69] Events would soon prove that this was naive optimism, but it may have been exactly what Robert Barnes thought about the situation although he did not write the letter.

The events which sealed the doom of Barnes began in Lent 1540, when he tactlessly and recklessly attacked a sermon of Stephen Gardiner, now Bishop of Winchester, and a leading figure in the Henrician Church.[70] Gardiner had delivered a sermon at Paul's Cross in which he lambasted the whole Protestant theology and especially justification by faith, the keystone of the Reformation. Barnes took the sermon as a challenge and proceeded to answer the bishop from the same pulpit two weeks later. In pointed manner and belligerent tone, Barnes set forth his Lutheran theology. This was quickly reported to the king who then summoned the offender to appear before him. Henry ordered Barnes and Gardiner to debate the issues in his presence, and when they did so, he decided in favor of Gardiner. Barnes was ordered to submit himself to the bishop for instruction to correct his errors. When Barnes proved uncooperative, Henry demanded a public recantation and apology to Gardiner.[71]

Now under heavy pressure from the throne, Barnes agreed to a public recantation, which was an opportunity to clear his name and perhaps even save his life. When the appointed time arrived, Barnes appeared as scheduled, but his address only further aggravated the situation. He did apologize and read a recantation of sorts, but its contents were so worded that he did not actually renounce any of his Lutheran beliefs. Moreover, before his address ended, he had uttered more remarks against Gardiner. Consequently, Barnes was imprisoned in the Tower, where he remained until his execution on 30 July 1540.[72] His conduct in the midst of this crisis assured his doom. It gave Henry the opportunity of "liquidating a servant who had outlived his usefulness."[73] By this time, the king had decided that he had no more use for Cromwell either. Nor did he need the Lutheran contacts which had been long associated with the names Barnes and Cromwell. Soon the two of them found their names on bills of attainder, charging them with heresy.

Cromwell's heresy consisted specifically of his co-operating with Barnes, especially in the circulation of heretical literature.[74]

Cromwell was not the only companion of Barnes who was indicted. Two fellow Protestants, Jerome and Garet, accompanied Barnes to the stake. They had long been associated with the efforts to reform the English Church. All three were branded as "detestable heretics [who] have openly preached erroneous opinions and perverted many texts of Scripture."[75] The final proceedings were vividly described by Edward Hall, the Henrician chronicler. Hall indicated that he had examined the attainder against the three Protestants, but that among the charges he could not ascertain which one was considered the warrant for their death. He believed that Bishop Gardiner was the one "who chiefly procured their death,"[76] a conclusion in which Foxe concurs.[77] Hall lamented that the accused seemed to be denied a fair trial. He complained that "suche learned menne should so bee cast a waie without examinacion, neither knowyng what was laied to their charge, nor never called to answere."[78]

At the stake Barnes affirmed his belief in all the historical doctrines of catholic Christianity as summarized in an ecumenical statement such as the *Apostles' Creed*. He added his commitment to a belief in the full sufficiency of Christ's death to make an atonement for sin, without human works of merit.[79] With a painful death approaching, Barnes is reported to have said to one of his companions in suffering: "Cheer up brother, today we shall be in glory."[80]

Predictably, Protestants on the Continent were outraged at the execution of Luther's English friend. Luther published a copy of Barnes' final confession at the stake. In his laudatory preface Luther referred to Barnes as "St. Robert," and Henry as "an incarnate devil."[81] Philip Melanchthon was so incensed he said, "there is no sacrifice more acceptable to God than the killing of a tyrant. Would that God might inspire some courageous man with this idea."[82]

Melanchthon's indignation can be understood, but his sentiments did not reflect Barnes' attitude toward his king either in life or death. This "loyal heretic" had been an untiring servant of his monarch and a champion of the royal supremacy throughout his public career. He had done all that could have reasonably been expected to accommodate himself to his ruler's wishes and still be true to his own conscience. His *Supplication unto King Henry* went through several revisions, and, each time, the changes show its author's willingness to support the political and ecclesiastical authority of the king in the circumstances of the changing times.[83] By 1530 Robert Barnes had become a throughgoing Lutheran in his beliefs, and from that date forward he was a heretic by Henry's standards. However, his Lutheranism mattered little to the king when Barnes' services were needed. Indeed, it was that very religious persuasion which the king found attractive. It was not until Dr. Barnes had outlived his usefulness that Henry found his theology intolerable. Clearly, Robert Barnes died a victim of expediency.

## WILLIAM TYNDALE (c. 1494-1536)

### Reformer-Humanist

In the opinion of Philip Hughes, one of the most respected Catholic authorities on the English Reformation, "William Tyndale [was] the greatest English light in the heretical firmament . . . and the most powerful solvent of English Catholicism since Wycliff."[84] . . . "The bishops and the king rightly regarded him as the gravest menace to the established order of things."[85]

The precise date and place of birth of William Tyndale have not been ascertained, though Foxe situates his birth at "the borders of Wales."[86] Likewise, little is known about his childhood and family background. The family name sometimes appeared as Hutchins and other times as Tyndale. Throughout his career he was often cited as Hutchins in letters and government documents, but apparently, Tyndale was the proper family name.[87]

The Tyndale family enjoyed a fairly prosperous rural life as middle-class farmers, thus making it possible for William to begin a university education at Oxford in 1506, when he was admitted to Magdalen Hall. Oxford University conferred upon him the degree of Bachelor of Arts in 1512 and the Master of Arts in 1515. Tyndale earned distinction as a student of divinity and the liberal arts, and, above all, as a linguist of phenomenal ability.[88]

By the time Tyndale began his university studies, Oxford had already experienced some of the impact of the new humanist scholarship begun by John Colet. The scholastic sophistries of the Scotists and Thomists had not disappeared from the university, but a new day for scholarship had dawned and was moving in the direction of its noontide brilliance. Tyndale allied himself with the new learning, and in his later polemical writings he reflected with contempt upon some of the scholastic debates he had witnessed at the university.[89] His great interest was in the application of textual scholarship to the study of the Bible, to which "his mind was singularly addicted; insomuch that he . . . read privily to certain students and fellows of Magdalen College, some parcel of divinity; instructing them in the knowledge and truth of the Scriptures."[90]

Sometime about 1519, Tyndale moved to Cambridge, which had by then surpassed Oxford as the great center of humanist education. Erasmus had taught at Cambridge from 1510-14, but there had been some resistance to his ideas. One college prohibited the use of his New Testament. In 1518, Richard Croke, formerly a professor at Leipzig, began to lecture at Cambridge on the Greek language. It may be that Tyndale was attracted to this university by Croke's reputation.[91]

It is also possible that Tyndale's interest in Cambridge was stimulated by the news that a controversy had erupted at the university regarding the question of indulgences, which was concurrently agitating Germany. Bishop John Fisher spoke for the established church by making defense of this practice. Tyndale remained at Cambridge until 1521, the year that Luther's writings were burned there.[92] By this time, he was an ordained priest, though the date and place of his ordination have not been verified.

Exactly what relations Tyndale maintained with the Cambridge reformers cannot be documented. However, he was there at a time when the White Horse circle of "Germans" was very active in the study and discussion of reformist ideas. Robert Barnes was then Austin prior, and, among others, Thomas Bilney, Hugh Latimer, and Thomas Cranmer were all part of the university community. It seems highly probable that Tyndale was associated with the White Horse group at some time during his sojourn at the university.

"Leaving that university also, he resorted to one Master Welch, a knight of Gloucestershire, and was there schoolmaster to his children, and in good favor with his master."[93] One can only conjecture why Tyndale left the university, but he spent 1522-23 as tutor to the children at Little Sodbury Manor, and it was there that he determined the goal of his life — to translate the Bible into English. The tutorial task was not terribly demanding for a scholar of Tyndale's ability, so he probably had considerable leisure to devote to his primary concern.[94]

Apparently, Tyndale's employer, Master Welch, enjoyed a fair degree of prestige among the clergy, for noted monastic and ecclesiastical figures were known to frequent his table. Among them were several doctors of theology. This gave William Tyndale opportunities to discuss the debated religious issues of the day with some learned contemporaries. The views of Luther and Erasmus were among the matters discussed; "also of diverse other controversies and questions upon the Scripture."[95] Master Tyndale regarded Erasmus as his spiritual mentor until he went to the Continent where he met Luther.[96]

Although he had not yet formally embraced Protestant views, while yet at Little Sodbury, Tyndale employed the humanist method of argumentation, which became the hallmark of all leading Protestant reformers; that is, he insisted that the settlement of doctrinal controversies required an appeal to the original source materials of Christianity — the Scriptures! He boldly confuted the sophistical arguments of visiting clerics by citing the Bible and, in so doing, made enemies among them. Despite the embarrassment that his disputatious manner must have caused Master Welch, Tyndale persisted until his employer and his wife were won over to the views of their tutor.[97]

From this time forward to the end of his life, Master Tyndale never ceased to cite the Bible as the final court of appeal in all spiritual matters. He believed that the Scriptures are sufficiently clear to settle all doctrinal controversies. His method of exegesis was to compare Scripture with

Scripture because, as he said, "the Scriptures, conferred together, expound themselves."[98]

Tyndale's opinions and manner of espousing them aroused strong clerical resentment, and, eventually, the offended churchmen ceased visiting Little Sodbury Manor. However, they did not discontinue their attacks upon their critic. For the rest of his life, Tyndale incurred the hostility and abuse of the defenders of the old order. His reaction was to become ever more anticlerical, often impugning both the sincerity and the scholarship of his opponents.

> This I suffer because the priests of the country are unlearned; as God knows it, they are a full ignorant sort, who have seen no more Latin than that they read in their portesses and missals, which yet many of them can scarcely read. . . . Therefore, . . . when they come together to the alehouse, which is their preaching place, they affirm that my sayings are heresy.[99]

Although Master Tyndale had drawn attention to himself by his advocacy of Biblical study and by his tirades against clerical ignorance, he had not yet published anything which might support his claim to scholarship. To meet this requirement, he decided to summon to his side the most renowned of all humanists — the great Erasmus. Erasmus was well known for his opposition to scholastic sophistries, and, like Tyndale, he was also an unrelenting critic of clerical ignorance and corruption. Therefore, Tyndale proposed to publish an English translation of Erasmus' *Enchiridion Militis Christiani* or *Handbook of the Christian Soldier,* which the "Prince of Humanists" had written in 1502 and revised in 1518. The *Enchiridion* had already aroused the animosity of priests who were offended by its uncomplimentary observations and conclusions. Now that Tyndale rendered it into English, the priestly party had additional cause to oppose him. Consequently, he was summoned to appear

ABOVE: Master William Tyndale  BELOW: Little Sodbury Manor, where Tyndale is thought to have begun translating the Bible.

before the Chancellor of Malvern to answer charges of heresy brought by those whom he had discomforted by his criticisms.[100] However, his judge found no evidence of heresy in Tyndale at that time.

The vigor of those who accused him only provoked Tyndale to become more outspoken and penetrating in his attacks on a clergy he regarded as corrupt. Soon after his hearing before the Chancellor of Malvern, Master Tyndale boldly denounced the papacy saying, "I defy the pope and all his laws," and, moreover, he vowed to make common plowboys more learned in the Scriptures than England's priests and prelates.

> After this, the grudge of the priests increasing still more and more against Tyndale, they never ceased barking and rating at him, and laid many things sorely at his charge, saying that he was a heretic in logic, a heretic in divinity.[101]

Tyndale always believed that the greatest obstacle to the spiritual health of England was its ignorance of Biblical teaching. His opinion was especially valid when applied to the region where he had lived, for, as Marcus Loane concludes, "the County of Gloucester was the most neglected Archdeaconry in the most neglected Diocese in all England."[102]

Therefore, just about the same time that Luther published his German New Testament (1522), Master William Tyndale decided to seek patronage which would allow him to complete the same task in the English vernacular. For this reason, he turned to Cuthbert Tunstal, Bishop of London. No doubt, Tyndale sought patronage from Tunstal because the bishop was known to be a Greek scholar who had studied in Italy and had made himself the friend of neo-classical scholars, and, notably, the close personal friend of Sir Thomas More.[103]

In order to impress Bishop Tunstal with his scholarship, Master Tyndale presented him with his English translation of a portion from the writings of Isocrates, the famed Athenian philosopher-educator. Since Erasmus had praised Tunstal as a true friend of learning, Tyndale fully expected to receive the bishop's support. To the contrary, however, Tunstal rejected the request, saying that he already had more residents in his household than he could comfortably support. In 1530, Tyndale mentioned his experience with the Bishop of London.

> But God (who knows what is within hypocrites) saw that I was beguiled, and that counsel was not the next way to my purpose. And therefore he got me no favour in my lord's sight. . . . I . . . understood at the last not only that there was no room in my lord of London's palace to translate the New Testament, but that there was no place to do it in all England, as experience does now openly declare.[104]

Tunstal was a cautious man who enjoyed the royal favor as Keeper of the Privy Seal. He would not jeopardize his position by lending support to a religious project which did not have the king's approval. He was one of those humanists "who laughed at the ignorance of the monks, but hesitated to touch an ecclesiastical system which lavished on them such rich sinecures."[105]

To Tyndale, this position did not reflect judicious caution but spineless cowardice. Therefore he branded the Bishop of London as a "still Saturn, that so seldom speaks but walks up and down all day musing and imagining mischief, a ducking hypocrite, made to dissemble."[106]

These vitriolic attacks on Tunstal were published in 1530, by which time the bishop had become an avowed enemy of the Protestant reformers in general and an opponent of their demand for an English Bible in particular. His agents had been confiscating and destroying heretical literature for some time. The result was that the bishop's "prisons were so full that he had to commit a fresh suspect to the Fleet."[107]

After being denied patronage by Tunstal, William Tyndale turned for help to Humphrey Monmouth, a rich merchant with whom he had recently established a friendship. Monmouth had a reputation for charity and was known to be sympathetic toward Evangelical ideas.[108] Apparently, Tyndale was supported by his rich friend for several months until he became convinced that he had to leave England in order to continue his project of producing an English Bible. "Finding no place for his purpose within the realm, and having, by God's providence, some aid and provision ministered unto him by Humphrey Monmouth . . . he took his leave of the realm, and departed into Germany."[109]

It is possible, and even likely, that Master Tyndale absorbed some elements of Lutheranism while in residence with Humphrey Monmouth. It appears, however, that both men still retained beliefs which stemmed from traditional medieval orthodoxy and were contrary to Evangelical principles. This is most evident in the testimony of Monmouth, who affirmed that he had given the priest Tyndale ten pounds to pray for his deceased parents and other departed souls.[110] The evidence seems conclusive. The William Tyndale who left England for Germany in 1524 was primarily a critic of clerical ignorance and ecclesiastical corruption —

an Erasmian scholar who saw instruction from the Scriptures as the best means to promote popular piety and Church reform. He was hardly yet a mature Protestant reformer. His experience to this point closely parallels that of Robert Barnes, who would begin his German exile in 1529.

## Reformer-Theologian

It has been remarked by a leading critic of the Reformation that William Tyndale

> has the immensely important place in the history
> of his country that he was the first influence in
> the formation of the English Protestant mind. He
> is so important that one is tempted to exaggerate
> and to say that he is the foundation on which all
> the rest has been built.[111]

Tyndale's great influence upon the molding of English Protestant thought came as the consequence of his own wholehearted conversion to the Evangelical cause. That conversion from Erasmian churchman to Protestant reformer, as was also the case with Robert Barnes, took place in Saxony, and probably under the direct personal influence of Martin Luther. After a brief stay in Hamburg, Tyndale went to Wittenberg, "where he had conference with Luther and other learned men in those quarters."[112] He had arrived in that city which Duke George of Saxony called "the common asylum of all apostates."[113]

While in Wittenberg, Tyndale seems to have completed his translation of the New Testament. Soon thereafter he began translating the Old Testament. By August 1525 Tyndale was in Cologne seeking a printer for his New Testament. He was now accompanied by William Roye, a renegade friar who had also been associated with Humphrey

Monmouth in England. Roye was "a man with a talent for boasting and indiscretion,"[114] and it may have been his unguarded tongue which brought their printing project to the attention of John Cochlaeus, a notorious enemy of the Reformation. Due to opposition from Cochlaeus, the project had to be moved from Cologne to Worms, where the work was completed in 1526 under the protection of the famed Lutheran prince, Philip of Hesse.

At last the indispensable tool for a truly evangelical reformation in England was made available to the zealots of that cause. Now, for the first time, it was possible for Englishmen so inclined to develop an English Protestant theology. Foremost among those of such inclination was William Tyndale himself.

Royal reaction to the publication of the English New Testament was violent. In his reply to Luther, Henry VIII expressed his feelings toward Tyndale, saying that Luther

> fell into device with one or two lewd persons, born in this our realm, for the translating of the New Testament into English, as well with many corruptions of that holy text, as certain prefaces in the margins, for the advancement and setting forth of abominable heresies.[115]

Dr. Edward Lee, almoner for the king, wrote to Henry from France on 2 December 1526:

> An Englishman, at the solicitation and instance of Luther, with whom he is, has translated the New Testament into English and within a few days intends to return with the same imprinted into England. I need not to advertise your Grace what infection and danger may ensue hereby if it is not withstood. This is the nearest way to fill your

realm full with Lutherans. For all Luther's opinions are grounded upon bare words of Scripture. . . . All our forefathers, governors of the Church of England, have with all diligence forbidden English Bibles. . . . The integrity of the Christian faith within your realm cannot long endure if these books may come in.[116]

Shortly before Lee's warning, Bishop Tunstal had preached at Paul's Cross where he denounced Tyndale's New Testament and presided over a burning of that work and other objectionable literature. About the same time, the English government tried unsuccessfully to prevent heretical books in English print from leaving Antwerp.[117] Apparently, the Merchant Adventurers carried Tyndale New Testaments to England. They had officers in Antwerp and Calais, and they traded with Hanse merchants who resided at the Steelyard where their Lutheranism had become proverbial. Those who patronized and smuggled Protestant books into England were so active that they have been called a "Forbidden Book of the Month Club."[118]

Bishop Tunstal made suppression of the vernacular New Testament a personal crusade. While on the Continent in 1529, he met Augustine Packington, a London cloth merchant, who agreed to aid him in acquiring a large number of Tyndale New Testaments to be consigned to the flames. In making this agreement, Packington was actually aiding Tyndale. For Packington

was a man that highly favored William Tyndale, but to the bishop utterly showed himself to the contrary. . . . The bishop thinking he had God by the toe, when indeed he had (as he thought after) the devil by the fist, said "gentle master Packing-

ton, do your diligence and get them, and with all
my heart I will pay for them, . . . for the books are
erroneous and naughty, and I intend surely to destroy them all, and to burn them at Paul's
Cross."[119]

Tyndale was glad to sell his copies of the New Testament
for burning, for thus he could pay his debts, and, at the
same time, the burning focused public attention on the destruction of the Scriptures. Moreover, the money realized
from the sale funded the needed revision of the New Testament.[120]

The public burnings of the New Testaments were merely
reflections of the combined hostility of the English Church
and state toward the Reformation, which became pronounced in the latter 1520's. As already noted, Robert
Barnes had been forced to do public penance in 1526, and
late in 1529 he had to flee to Germany. Cardinal Wolsey's
agents in the Low Countries were still achieving almost
nothing in their efforts to impede the printing of the New
Testament. By 1530 Luther's writings in translation, together with the English New Testament, were being cir-
culated through England in quantity. The Bishop of Norwich admitted with a sense of frustration that there was no
effective way to thwart it. Apparently, there was a significant level of literacy in England. The very censorship im-
posed by church and state shows the potential power of the
printed word.

Having laid the foundation with his New Testament, Tyndale next led the way in erecting the doctrinal structure of
an English Protestantism by the theological exposition of
the sacred text he had made available to the English reading public. In rapid succession, Tyndale composed and published those treatises which became the cornerstone for an

English Reformed faith. In 1527, he wrote *The Parable of the Wicked Mammon*, an exposition of the doctrine of justification by faith in the manner of Martin Luther. Later in the same year, he issued a ringing affirmation of his faith in the royal supremacy in *The Obedience of a Christian Man. The Practice of Prelates,* his most polemical work, appeared in 1530, as did his prologues to the Pentateuch. Parallel with these efforts, Tyndale wrote expository prologues to almost every book of the New Testament.

It will be necessary to consider each of Tyndale's major writings as they express his views on the great doctrinal issues which agitated the Reformation era. In doing so, it will become apparent that recent scholarship is divided over the question of making an exact identification of the particular stream of Protestant thought for which Tyndale was the major English spokesman. It is the opinion of this present writer that the conclusion of E. G. Rupp, with a few qualifications, is the most convincing. "Tyndale was a reformer; in all great matters save perhaps in the doctrine of the eucahristic presence he agreed with Martin Luther."[121]

"These books of William Tyndale being compiled, published, and sent over into England, it cannot be spoken what a door of light they opened to . . . the whole English nation, which before were many years shut up in darkness."[122] In thus stating his conviction, Foxe obviously did not speak for the entire nation, as the opposition of ranking clergymen such as Bishop Tunstal indicates. Moreover, Sir Thomas More had already begun a literary crusade against Protestant heresy. His theological duel with Tyndale would become one of the most famous debates of their epoch. This was initiated when Tunstal gave More license to read heretical books for the purpose of composing rebuttals in the vernacular. More even sent his books to the Continent in the hope of combatting the Protestant enterprise at its source.[123]

Throughout the period in which he was engaged in controversy with the defenders of the old religious order, Tyndale repeatedly emphasized his unswerving loyalty to Henry VIII. He knew that the attitude of the king might be crucial for the future prospects of the Reformation at home, so he appealed to the ruler from his exile abroad. Tyndale's affirmation of the Biblical basis for civil obedience pleased Henry so much that he said of *The Obedience of a Christian Man*, "this is a book for me and all kings to read."[124]

Tyndale's profession of loyalty and his evident literary abilities greatly impressed Thomas Cromwell, Henry's chief minister, who then persuaded the king to try to enlist Tyndale as a pamphleteer for the royal cause. Stephen Vaughan, Cromwell's agent on the Continent, was to be the mediator, as he would be also in the recruitment of Robert Barnes soon thereafter. Tyndale's help was solicited for use against the clergy, but his stubborn opposition to the royal divorce caused the king to cease his solicitations. When *The Practice of Prelates* appeared (1530) with its denial of Henry's case against Catherine of Aragon, the king lost all interest in Tyndale's possible usefulness. Tyndale was virtually the only major English reformer to oppose the divorce, a fact which must have made Henry all the more angry with him. Cromwell's letter to Vaughan of 20 May 1531 reflects the king's change of mood.

> The king considers that if he (Tyndale) were present he would probably do what he could to infect and corrupt the whole realm, to the great inquietation and hurt of the commonwealth.[125]

Tyndale had told Vaughan that he would cease writing if

only the king would permit the publication of a vernacular Bible without marginal notes.[126]

Much of the time that William Tyndale was on the Continent he was a man on the move. Sometimes he had to travel in order to find a printer for his books. At other times he was a refugee fleeing from the Catholic authorities who had branded him a dangerous disseminator of heresy. Nevertheless, for most of the last eight years of his life (1528-36) Tyndale seems to have used the city of Antwerp as his base of operations. There he was in touch with people coming from home, and his association with the English merchant community provided a means to smuggle his books and Bibles into his homeland.

As Tyndale continued producing theological treatises and translations of selected Old Testament books, the government in England stiffened its posture of resistence to the Reformation. In 1530 a decree had been read throughout the land. It was entitled "A Proclamation for the resisting and withstanding of most damnable Heresies, sown within this Realm by the Disciples of Luther, and other Heretics, perverters of Christ's Religion."[127] The year 1531 brought stringent efforts to implement its provisions against religious nonconformity. In this effort, conservative prelates such as Archbishop Warham, and Bishops John Stokesley and Cuthbert Tunstal joined with Lord Chancellor Thomas More in pressing the hunt for heretics.

Warham presided over a royal commission invested with the authority and responsibility of suppressing religiously objectionable literature. The translations and treatises of Master Tyndale were high on the list of items marked for destruction. Conservative clerics dominated the commission, although it did contain a minority who favored legalizing the publication of the Scriptures in the vernacular.

The most prominent advocate of the English Bible at this time was Hugh Latimer, the university preacher at Cambridge, who enjoyed the royal favor at the moment because of his fervent support of the king's case for an annulment from Queen Catherine. On 1 December 1530 Latimer wrote an impassioned plea asking the king to authorize the use of the Scripture in the common tongue.[128] His plea fell on deaf ears, and Latimer had to conduct himself with extreme caution lest he incur the suspicion of heresy. Hugh Latimer proved himself quite dexterous in the art of survival amid the turbulent tides of ecclesiastical life for the rest of this reign.

The personal good fortune of Latimer notwithstanding, the decade of the 1530's brought increasing trouble to those sympathetic toward the Reformation. Attempts to ban Protestant books were never very effective, but those apprehended for circulating them were now in acute danger. Thomas Bilney, who had been instrumental in leading both Barnes and Latimer toward the Evangelical faith, was burnt in Norwich at the Lollard's Pit about mid-1531.[129] He was soon followed in death by John Lambert, once chaplain to the English merchants at Antwerp. By this time, Robert Barnes had returned to England, and Chancellor More was seeking a way to effect his arrest.

The persecution in the homeland was soon extended abroad. Sir Thomas Elyot was dispatched as ambassador to the imperial court with orders to seek the arrest of Tyndale and his extradition to England. Elyot wrote to Cromwell on 18 November 1532 complaining that his ambassadorial duties and the cost of seeking Tyndale were causing him to sink deeply into debt: "I spent money to gain knowledge, especially to those by whom I trusted to apprehend Tyndale according to the King's commandment."[130] Meanwhile, in the hope of discovering the whereabouts of Tyndale, More interrogated people who had recently been to Antwerp.[131]

Once it became evident that Elyot was unable to obtain effective assistance from the government of the Low Countries, Henry VIII personally appealed to Charles V to aid in the capture of Tyndale. Henry did this despite the fact that he and Charles were on bad terms because of Henry's divorce of Catherine of Aragon, the emperor's aunt.[132] Apparently, Tyndale was the beneficiary of this animosity between the rulers, for Charles' lack of enthusiasm to co-operate with Henry probably allowed the reformer a few more years of freedom. However, the end was approaching for England's foremost reformer-theologian.

## Reformer-Martyr

By 1533, Tyndale was fully aware that the partisans of the Reformation were in grave danger in a number of places. He reported knowing of brethren who had recently perished for their faith in Antwerp, Flanders, Rouen, and Paris.[133] However, the one whose suffering grieved Tyndale most must have been his beloved friend and comrade in the cause of the Reformation, John Frith. Frith was another Cambridge scholar who had fled to the Continent after espousing the Evangelical faith. He was a polished author in his own right, and, at one time, Cromwell and Vaughan had sought unsuccessfuly to make him a royal propagandist also. For a while, Frith used his exile to write on Reformed doctrinal themes and to answer attacks by Thomas More and Bishop John Fisher.[134] But Frith could not endure a long separation from England, so he returned in August 1532. Although he tried to remain inconspicuous, his fame as an expositor of Scripture spread quickly, and his activities came to the attention of his arch enemy, Thomas More.

Frith was imprisoned in the Tower of London as a heretic because of his published denials of transubstantiation and purgatory. He perished in the flames at Smithfield on 4 July 1533. Tyndale wrote to encourage Frith in the hour of trial. "Fear not men that threaten, nor trust men that speak fair; but trust him that is true of promise, and able to make his word good. Your cause is Christ's Gospel, a light that must be fed with the blood of faith."[135]

Although Thomas More retired from the chancellorship in 1532, he continued to write energetically against heretics, especially against William Tyndale and Robert Barnes, for whom he had an intense dislike. He called Barnes "a child of everlasting damnation," and Tyndale "that hellhound of the devil's kennel."[136] Ironically, More preceded both of these reformers in martyrdom, but his death brought no great respite to the propagators of Protestantism.

In 1534 Tyndale issued the revised version of his New Testament. Textual changes were relatively few, but some of the most polemical marginal notes of the first edition were omitted. He was now residing in Antwerp as a guest of Thomas Poyntz, a member of the English merchant community in the city. There Tyndale continued to write, while also performing many deeds of charity in the city and rendering some spiritual ministries to Englishmen interested in Reformation teachings.[137]

Late in 1535, some advocates of the English Reformation thought they had reason for optimism. In October an English edition of the Bible compiled on the Continent by Myles Coverdale, former secretary to Robert Barnes at Cambridge, was endorsed by Thomas Cromwell and approved for reading in England. No doubt, the favorable reception given to this version was related to the complete absence of marginal glosses with a sectarian slant. Then too, papal authority had been utterly rejected by the established Church by this time.[138] Coverdale had once been a member of the White Horse circle and had spent time with Tyndale when the latter was translating the five books of Moses.[139]

Although the state's permission to circulate a vernacular Bible was a monumental victory for the reformers, it did not mark the end of persecution. William Tyndale was still in danger, and the agent of his destruction was already moving against him.

Sometime in 1535, one Henry Phillips had appeared at Antwerp. It seems that he had fled from his father in England after losing a large sum of his father's money gambling. Or, it may be that he stole money from his father and fled to the Continent to spend it. Whatever the case, he then sought a position in the service of Charles V. Phillips wanted to apprehend Tyndale as a means of gaining favorable notice from the emperor. He led Tyndale into a trap by inviting him out to dine, only to deliver him into the hands of imperial agents. Phillips later failed in two attempts to apprehend Robert Barnes. Tyndale became a prisoner at the Vilvorde fortress in May 1535, and remained there until his death the next year.[140]

The seizure of Tyndale was a great blow to Thomas Poyntz, his host. Apparently, Poyntz felt that the English government, or at least Cromwell, should try to intercede on Tyndale's behalf. In August 1535, Poyntz wrote to his brother John in England:

> As Tyndale has lived in my house three quarters of a year, I know that the King has no truerhearted subject living, for he knows he is bound by the law of God to obey his Prince. He would not do contrary to be lord of the world, however the king is

> informed. . . . The death of this man will be a great
> hindrance to the gospel, and to the enemies of it
> one of the highest pleasures. . . .
>
> Therefore I desire you that this matter may be
> solicited to his grace for this man, . . . for in my
> conscience there are not many more perfect men
> living . . . as God knows.[141]

Stephen Vaughan believed that a letter from Cromwell
could save Tyndale's life. Actually, Cromwell had moved to
aid Tyndale even before receiving this appeal from
Vaughan. Henry's chief minister wrote to two ranking no-
bles on the privy council of Brabant, forwarding the letters
to Vaughan for delivery.[142] Vaughan in turn entrusted delivery to Poyntz who was very anxious to help his imprisoned friend. The letters did not achieve their intended end,
and their bearer Poyntz was accused by Henry Phillips of
being a Tyndalian heretic. Consequently, the unfortunate
Poyntz was arrested and held for over three months until he
managed to escape to England.[143] He left his possessions,
business interests, and his wife and children behind.

In August 1536, Master William Tyndale was deprived of
Holy Orders and remanded to the civil authorities for execution as an incorrigible heretic. He endured a martyr's death
sometime during the following October, "strangled first by
the hangman, and . . . afterwards with fire consumed, . . .
crying with . . . a loud voice, 'Lord! Open the king of England's eyes' "[144] Hall's chronicle reported that even the imperial procurator general who prosecuted his case admitted
that Tyndale was "learned, godly, and good."[145]

In life William Tyndale was unique among the early English reformers in that he was their only great original
expositor of Scripture. Robert Barnes mainly served as an

English mediator of Luther's ideas, some of his works being paraphrases of the great German reformer. Others, such as Coverdale, concentrated on translating Continental authors. Tyndale was also unique among his peers in death. During the reign of Henry VIII, all the great men of the Reformation recanted at some point to save their lives. This was the case with Bilney, Barnes, Frith, Latimer, and others, but not so with Tyndale. His courage never failed, and he deserves recognition as the most constant reformer of his generation. Foxe reported that while in prison, Tyndale converted his jailer and some of the jailer's family.[146]

Religious persecution seldom accomplishes the designs of its architects. In sixteenth century Europe, "the smoke of the fires which consumed the martyrs seemed to infect all upon whom it blew."[147] Tragically, the civil and ecclesiastical authorities were distressingly slow in comprehending this. Consequently,

> freedom of conscience there was none. Tolerance was proclaimed an emanation of Hell. Difference of opinion was deadly. To acknowledge misgiving or doubt or dissent was incontinently to be rated as a rebel and exposed to the truculency of a pitiless hierarchy.[148]

Although his enemies destroyed his life, they were powerless to defeat Tyndale's influence. Like Luther, he wrote in a style that all of his literate countrymen could understand. The products of his pen were compiled together with those of Robert Barnes and John Frith in 1573. These writings were the first bricks laid upon the foundation of the English New Testament, the greatest fruit of Tyndale's labors.

## CHAPTER 3

# THE QUESTION OF AUTHORITY

## THE NATURE OF THE PROBLEM

Throughout history, the tranquility of visible Christendom has been repeatedly disturbed by the appearance and propagation of doctrinal and moral concepts deemed to be incompatible with that body of teaching which had come to be accepted as the norm. Never were the dimensions of such disturbance so great as in the sixteenth century, when the Protestant reformers demanded that more than a thousand years of ecclesiastical tradition stand trial before the bar of the open Bible. The nature of God and man, salvation and the sacraments, as well as church and state, were all furiously debated between the reformers and the defenders of medieval orthodoxy. At the root of every such dispute was the fundamental issue of authority. By what authority are these controversies to be settled?

Since the twelfth century, a vast body of ecclesiastical regulations had been codified in the canon law, which was based upon the Bible, the writings of the Church Fathers, the decrees of synods and councils and the decrees of the popes. This corpus was regarded as the authoritive repository of tradition and, therefore, the standard of judgment in moral and theological controversies.[1]

Almost from the moment of its codification, there were sporadic expressions of discontent with the exalted status accorded to canon law. Late medieval movements such as the Waldensees and Hussites on the Continent and the Lollards in England challenged the supremacy of canon law by their insistence upon direct appeal to the text of the Bible as the authority for their deviations from established dogma. These sects did obtain a significant following for a while, and, in some measure, they survived into the sixteenth century despite savage persecution. But their impact was less than revolutionary. They never gained sufficient numbers to be regarded as anything more than pestiferous splinter factions by church and state alike.

As we noted in reference to the Lollards, the germs of most theological tenets of the sixteenth century reformers are already evident in the doctrines advanced by their late medieval precursors.[2] This is especially apparent in their anticlericalism, as well as their fervent commitment to Biblical authority. But while their precursors were barely able to endure the wrath of the ecclesiastical reaction which they provoked, the sixteenth century reformers unleashed a flood of change which permanently altered the face of Christendom.

No doubt, a number of factors must be considered in appraising the reasons for Protestantism's sweeping successes in the sixteenth century. Paramount among them, however, was the availability of what Foxe called "the divine and miraculous invention of printing."[3] Even those who do not admit the providential view held by Foxe cannot deny that the invention of the printing press was a factor of monumental importance in assuring the success of the Protestant enterprise. Beginning with Luther, every major Evangelical reformer became either a pamphleteer or a translator, or both. So it is not difficult to understand why Foxe concluded that "either the pope must abolish printing, or . . . printing doubtless will abolish him."[4]

By the time that Luther's students began circulating copies of his *Ninety-five Theses,* printing by means of movable type had been in use for more than half a century. And the level of literacy was rising across western Europe. This meant that it was now possible to conduct theological debates on an unprecedented scale and to involve thousands of informed supporters as partisans in the controversies. This is precisely what occurred. The Protestant reformers invited Christendom to make a first-hand examination of the Bibles which they were publishing in the vernacular. In earlier times calling men back to the Scriptures had only a limited effect, for few Bibles existed and the vast majority of people could not read. With the advent of the printing press, this condition was dramatically changed.

Long before the printing press made possible the mass circulation of the Scriptures, the medieval Church had recognized that private possession and use of the Bible in the vernacular tongues might well abet the spread of doctrinal disaffection. Consequently, beginning in the thirteenth century, the Church moved to forbid laymen to read the Bible in their vulgar language. Evidently the first official action of this kind was a prohibitory decree of the Council of Toulouse in 1229.[5]

A ban on the use of vernacular Scriptures in England came as part of the clerical reaction to the endeavors of John Wyclif. In 1409 the English Church met in convocation at Oxford, where Thomas Arundel, Archbishop of Canterbury, promulgated a constitution of thirteen articles. The seventh article specifically connected the English Bible with heresy.

> We ... decree and ordain, that no man, hereafter,
> by his own authority translate any text of the

Scripture into English or any other tongue, by way of a book, libel, or treatise; and that no man read any such book, libel, or treatise, now lately set forth in the name of John Wickliff, ... upon pain of greater excommunication, until the said translation be allowed by the ordinary of the place, or ... by the council provincial. He that shall do contrary to this, shall likewise be punished as a favourer of error and heresy.[6]

Historically, the medieval Church recognized the Bible as one authoritative source for her doctrinal and moral teachings, but she granted neither the exclusive authority of the Scriptures nor the right of private individuals to interpret them. The reformers of the sixteenth century insisted on the sole authority of the Scriptures and demanded for themselves the prerogative of individual interpretation. The printing press gave them the means to make their demand effective. Prominent among the champions of *sola scriptura* and the vernacular Bible were Robert Barnes and William Tyndale, both of whom deserve recognition as fathers of the English Reformation, because they held the conviction that "if the clergy conceal the light, the layman must have his own Bible. . . . The Christian must go straight to the Bible, trusting the Holy Spirit to interpret it to him."[7]

## ROBERT BARNES ON AUTHORITY

On Christmas Day, 1537, Hugh Latimer wrote to Thomas Cromwell:

Mr. Doctor Barnes has preached here with me at Hartlebury, and at my request at Winchester, and also at Evesham. Surely he is alone in handling a piece of scripture, and in setting forth of Christ he

has no fellow. I would that the king's grace might
once hear him.[8]

Although the distinction of being the greatest linguist
and expositor of Scripture in the early English Reformation
belongs to William Tyndale, credit is due to Robert Barnes
as an especially gifted preacher and pamphleteer. The
above commendation from Latimer was corroborated by an
interesting episode which reflects Barnes' impact as a pul-
piteer.

On 23 November 1537 Humphrey Monmouth, Tyndale's
benefactor, died in London where he had been an alderman.
In his last will and testament, Monmouth ignored the custom of designating a sum of money to have thirty masses
said for the repose of his soul. Instead, he endowed the
preaching of thirty sermons by four advocates of the Evangelical faith. Foremost among the designated preachers was
Dr. Robert Barnes.[9]

Barnes' zeal for preaching the Evangelical doctrines grew
out of his firm conviction that these were the teachings of
the Scriptures, for which he had the highest regard. As a
mature Lutheran theologian, he echoed the cry of the Wittenberg Reformer for *sola scriptura*. Like Luther, Barnes favored the circulation of the Bible in the vernacular. Therefore he boldly assailed the English bishops who condemned
Tyndale's version of the New Testament while producing
none of their own. In the second edition of his *Supplication
unto King Henry VIII* (1534), Barnes expounded his views on
this subject in an article entitled "That it is lawfull for all
manner of men to read the holy Scripture." His biting remarks were addressed to the bishops.

How can Antichrist be better known, than by this
token, that he condemns [the] Scriptures and

makes it heresy and high treason against the king's grace for laymen to read holy Scripture?[10]

Barnes categorically accused the episcopal opponents of the English Bible of suppressing the vernacular Scripture because it would expose their hypocrisies. "The truth was therein which you could not abide for men to know. . . . I say to you, if you do not amend it shall be to your everlasting damnation; for God will not take this rebuke at your hand."[11] For Barnes, the example of Christ should settle the issue of whether or not to allow laymen direct access to the Scriptures. "Our Master sent the Pharisees to the scriptures, and you forbid Christian men to read them."[12]

Although the law of the established Church forbade unauthorized Bible translations, Barnes believed that he had the sanction of a higher authority to encourage the use of the Scripture in the English language. He appealed to the Bible itself as attesting to the need to make its text available in the language of the common people. His point was that, if laymen ought not to read the Scriptures, why were they addressed to lay readers originally? Barnes reminded his critics that within the Biblical record itself there are examples of laymen expounding Old Testament portions to people of the New Testament era. Specifically, he cited the case of Aquila and Priscilla narrated in the Acts of the Apostles, Chapter 18.[13]

Likewise, Barnes argued, the Apostle Paul, in 2 Timothy 3:15, 16, said that the Scriptures are the means to educate people in the ways of God. "Paul says it is good to inform, and to instruct in righteousness; and you bishops say to inform produces heresy."[14]

John Standish of Whittington College, London, was one of the most bitter foes of Robert Barnes. Shortly after Barnes' execution in 1540, Standish published a violent treatise in which he attempted to refute the final confession of faith uttered by Barnes at the stake.[15] The appearance of this polemic aroused Myles Coverdale to rise to the defense of his former Austin prior with a rebuttal. In his answer to Standish, Coverdale reported that Standish attacked Barnes because the latter "would never willingly grant anything but what is in scripture."[16]

The charge was quite accurate, for Barnes did make the Bible his final arbiter in all disputes with his theological opponents. Nevertheless, Barnes was also adept in the use of the Church Fathers. Since his Catholic opponents regarded the Fathers as a source of authority adjunct to the Scriptures, Barnes enlisted St. Augustine and St. Athanasius, among others, to fortify his arguments in favor of laymen reading the Bible in their common tongue. Still controverting his episcopal adversaries, Barnes wrote:

> St. Augustine moves men to read holy Scripture; and you command them not to read it. St. Augustine says: "They shall know in them what to do, and what not to do," and you say they shall learn nothing therefrom but heresies. St. Augustine says: "a man without learning of scriptures, is no better than a brute beast"; are you not good fathers that will make all your children no better than beasts?

St. Athanasius provided especially persuasive support:

> "If you wish that your children shall be obedient . . . give them the words of God. But you shall not say that it belongs only to religious men to study Scriptures; but rather it belongs to every Chris-

tian man, and especially to him that is wrapped
[up] in the business of this world."[17]

Robert Barnes never ceased blaming the episcopacy for
the religious and civil difficulties which afflicted England.
He shared Tyndale's belief that ignorance of Biblical teaching was the root cause of most of his country's problems.
Since Archbishop Arundel had issued his constitution in
1409, translation of the Bible had been the exclusive
prerogative of the bishops. Because the prelates had not
only failed to produce an authorized version but had also
condemned the effort of Tyndale, Barnes was unsparing in
assailing them.

> If you do not revoke the condemnation of the New
> Testament, and ordain that all Christian men
> may read holy Scripture, you shall have the great-
> est shame that ever man had in this world. . . . You
> worms' meat, you stinking carrion, you nourish-
> ment of hell fire, how dare you thus presume
> against your God omnipotent.[18]

During the two centuries preceding the appearance of the
Protestant challenge, the medieval Church had been convulsed by a bitter internal quarrel over the matter of the
primacy of spiritual authority. The controversy was provoked by the "Great Schism," which featured a split in the
College of Cardinals leading to the establishment of rival
pontifical sees at Rome and Avignon from 1378-1417. The
rivals decreed mutual excommunications, and all of Christendom was required to choose sides between them.

After all attempts at persuasion failed to resolve the dispute, the theologians at the University of Paris proposed
that a general council of the Church decide the matter before the scandal caused irreparable damage. Consequently,

the conciliar movement convened a general council at Pisa in 1409. However, the opposing claimants to the papal throne refused to acknowledge its decisions, so the pope chosen by the council merely became the third contestant.

In 1414, the Holy Roman Emperor Sigismund convened a council at Constance. By this time, Catholic opinion was thoroughly disgusted with the divided Church, so Constance succeeded in removing all three contending popes and electing a single pontiff.

The Great Schism was ended, but the manner in which the dispute had been resolved raised another problem. Since a general council had restored order to the papacy, did primacy of authority reside with the papacy or the council? This is a question which has not been resolved to the satisfaction of all Catholics to the present day, though a long period of papal monarchy was initiated by the Counter-Reformation.

During the crucial years of Catholic-Protestant debate in the sixteenth century, the reformers had to address themselves to the issue of conciliar vs. Biblical authority. No one ever set forth the reformers' position more boldly than Luther in his famed address to the Diet of Worms (1521).

> Unless I am convinced by the testimony of the Scriptures or by clear reason (for I do not trust either in the pope or in councils alone, since it is well known that they have often erred and contradicted themselves), I am bound by the Scriptures I have quoted and my conscience is captive to the Word of God. I cannot and will not retract anything, since it is neither safe nor right to go against conscience.[19]

Robert Barnes echoed Luther's sentiments in even more pungent tones.

> Before the dreadful throne of God shall the council be judged by Christ's holy word, and Christ shall not be judged by the decree of the council, but He shall be the council's judge.[20]

In typical Lutheran fashion, Barnes insisted that popes, councils, Church Fathers and scholastic theologians be subjected to the arbitrament of Scripture. In taking this position, Barnes was not reacting blindly to a body of writings of which he was basically ignorant. To the contrary, it appears that his knowledge of the patristic and scholastic theologians excelled that of any other early English reformer.[21] Barnes' *Sententiae* reveal broad acquaintance with the Church Fathers, and his other essays show that he was conversant with the schoolmen.

Throughout his theological writings Robert Barnes consistently regarded the Scriptures as the Word of God, and therefore his confidence in the authority of the sacred text was unbounded. He was fond of asserting that the words of Scripture were "written by the Holy Ghost."[22] Barnes equated the Word of God with the words of Scripture.[23] He concluded: "to take away [the] scriptures from laymen is as much as to take Christ away from them."[24] Barnes never composed a detailed, definitive treatise on the precise nature and extent to which the Biblical authors were inspired by God, but the constant use of the Bible to prove his own arguments and to refute those of his opponents presupposes his utter confidence in the trustworthiness of Scripture. Consequently, the conclusion seems justified that Barnes viewed the Bible as "the only infallible source of religious knowledge" and accepted it as the inspired Word of God.[25]

Although Martin Luther exalted the authority of Scripture over tradition and contemporary papal pronouncements, he at first questioned the canonicity of the Epistles to the Hebrews and of James and Jude and the book of the Revelation.[26] Luther is quoted as having a particular disdain for the Epistle of James. The following remarks were recorded by his table guest Casper Heydenreich in 1542:

> We should throw the Epistle of James out of this school [Wittenberg University], for it doesn't amount to much. It contains not a syllable about Christ. . . . I maintain that some Jew wrote it who probably heard about Christian people but never encountered any.[27]

In the first edition of his preface to the New Testament (1522), Luther expressed his dislike for James. At the same time, he gave pointed expression to his Christocentric exegetical presupposition:

> In a word St. John's Gospel and his first epistle, St. Paul's epistles, especially Romans, Galatians, and Ephesians, and St. Peter's first epistle are the books that show you Christ and teach you all that is necessary and salvatory for you to know, even if you were never to see or hear any other book or doctrine. Therefore, St. James' epistle is really an epistle of straw, compared to these others, for it has nothing of the nature of the gospel about it.[28]

But it should be noted that Luther did, in fact, include James (as well as Hebrews, Jude, and Revelation) at the end of his New Testament — and that he did *not* include the above quotation in subsequent editions of his preface to the New Testament. Although Luther did not identify James as one of the Apostles, he did finally acknowledge the canonicity of the epistle.

Dr. Robert Barnes was surely the most thoroughly Lutheran theologian among the major English reformers, and in the original version of his *Supplication unto King Henry VIII* he argued against accepting the canonicity of James.[29] However, the later editions of the *Supplication* omit the disparagement of James altogether. Evidently, in his mature thought, Barnes recognized the same canon of Scripture which had been acknowledged since the ancient Church.

Once they had committed themselves to the authority of the Bible as opposed to tradition, the reformers were still faced with the matter of how the Bible was to be interpreted properly. Here again, Luther led the way; Barnes and others followed.

Scriptural exegetes in the medieval Church worked on the assumption that there were four senses in which the Biblical texts were to be understood: 1) the literal; 2) the allegorical — deriving spiritual applications for the Church; 3) the tropological — deriving moral lessons for the Christian's life; and 4) the anagogical, or eschatological.[30] Luther never abandoned any of these approaches completely, but he gave priority to the literal-historical sense. At the same time, his view of Scripture was always Christocentric.

Luther's influence on the exegesis of other reformers was ponderous. Both Barnes and Tyndale stressed that precedence must be given to the literal-historical sense, both held to the Christocentric perspective, and both believed that the clear meaning of the text may best be ascertained by comparing Scripture with Scripture.

Barnes' exegetical method must be gleaned from his polemical writings, since, unlike Tyndale, he did not produce any systematic expositions of the books of the Bible. In a portion of his *Supplication* entitled "Faith only justifieth before God," Barnes addressed himself to the interpretive problem posed by the apparent discrepancy between St. Paul and St. James on the matter of just what it is that gives a sinful man right standing before the holy God. Paul said that the sinner is justified (declared righteous) by faith in Christ, but James declared that a man is justified by faith *and* good works. We shall deal with the intricacies of this matter in more detail in the chapter on salvation. However, it is appropriate at this point to raise the issue as an illustration of Barnes' method of Biblical interpretation.

Robert Barnes finally accepted the canonicity of James and chose a means of reconciling him with St. Paul. Barnes enunciated his exegetical principle in this way:

> Wherefore seeing that there appears a controversy here in two places of the scripture, it stands with all reason, and learning, that the same place, which seems to be most feeble and also darkest (obscure), should be expounded and declared, by that part of scripture, that is clearest and of most authority.... For in all the scripture is not this article of justification so plainly and plenteously handled, as it is by blessed St. Paul. This every learned man must grant. Therefore it stands with reason and learning, that this saying of St. James must be reduced, and brought unto blessed St. Paul's meaning, and not St. Paul unto St. James' saying.[31]

Barnes obviously did not regard all books of the Bible as being of equal value for doctrinal instruction. But his particular position was that the incidental portions of Scripture must be interpreted in the light of the systematic ones. In the case in point, Paul was the systematic teacher on justification, so James must be understood in a sense that will not contradict him.

Robert Barnes felt that St. Augustine had found the ideal way to harmonize Paul and James. According to Augustine, Paul wrote of one's justification before God, whereas James dealt with justification before men. Therefore, a man's righteous standing before God is solely by faith in Christ, but good works are the necessary fruits of justification to other men, as James correctly taught. "St. James speaks of works that follow faith."[32] This interpretation was also officially subscribed to by Luther and accepted by Philip Melanchthon, who incorporated it in his *Apology of the Augsburg Confession* under the subheading "Reply to the Opponents' Arguments."[33]

This reconciliation of Paul and James had several important advantages for the Protestant polemicist. First, it preserved intact the great Reformation imperative of justification before God *sola fide*. Second, by citing Augustine, it strengthened the reformers' claim that their doctrine was a restoration of the teaching of the ancient Church. Third, it helped to rebut the Roman Catholic charge that the Evangelicals discounted the importance of good works and encouraged moral laxity. Finally, because of his view of justification Barnes could not be legitimately accused of tampering with the established canon of Scripture.

In addition to advocating an essentially literal-historical approach to the Bible as ordered by their Christocentric motif, the reformers tended to emphasize that the proper understanding of Scripture required the tutorial guidance of the Holy Spirit, its primary author. John Frith, Barnes' friend and fellow martyr, spoke for his generation of Protestant Bible scholars when he wrote:

> St. Peter says, that the scripture is not expounded
> after the appetite of any private person, but even
> as it was given, by the Spirit of God and not by
> men's will. So must it be declared by the same
> Spirit.[34]

As will be seen subsequently, this was a view in which
William Tyndale concurred heartily. Oddly, Robert Barnes'
writings make no mention of the Holy Spirit as an illumi-
nator for the student of the Bible, although it is highly probable that he believed in this concept, at least formally.

To summarize then, Dr. Robert Barnes, the most Lutheran of all the major English reformers, was an unswerving
exponent of the Protestant principle of *sola scriptura* — the
Bible only as the supreme arbiter of doctrine and morals.
With Luther and Tyndale, he appealed vigorously for the
use of Scripture in the vernacular, and, like these comrades
in the cause of the reform, saw Christ as the central figure
of all Scripture, the Old Testament as well as the New.


## WILLIAM TYNDALE ON AUTHORITY

Throughout his theological and expository writings, William Tyndale repeatedly and unequivocally committed himself to the supreme authority of the Bible and insisted that
would-be ecclesiastical leaders submit to the judgment of
the sacred text.

> In the kingdom of Christ, and in his Church or
> congregation, and in his councils, the ruler is the
> scripture, approved through the miracles of the
> Holy Spirit, and men are only servants; and Christ
> is the head, we all brethren.[35]

Moreover, Tyndale held that a church leader who violates the Word of God should be removed, for "his brethren have authority by the scripture to put him down, and to send him out of Christ's Church among the heretics, who prefer their false doctrine above the true word of Christ."[36] Tyndale exempted no one, least of all the pope, from this dictum.

The literary duel between Tyndale and Sir Thomas More was fought largely over the issue of authority for the Christian faith. In the midst of their debate, Tyndale challenged More and all of his other opponents to judge all claimants to spiritual authority solely on the basis of Scripture.

> Judge, therefore, reader whether the pope with his (clerics) are the church; whether their authority be above the scripture; whether all they teach without scripture be equal with the scripture.[37]

By urging Christian laymen to use the Scripture as a standard with which to gauge the piety and performance of the pope and his clergy, Tyndale was, in effect, calling for a radical reversal of ecclesiastical priorities. The canon lawyers and theologians of the late medieval Church may have been divided over the question of papal vs. conciliar primacy, but they were unanimous in rejecting the Protestant plea for *sola scriptura*.

The adamant position of the clergy against the Reformation concept of authority provoked Tyndale to accelerate and accentuate his efforts to bring the entire clerical establishment to trial at the tribunal of the open Bible. He urged the readers of the *Parable of the Wicked Mammon* (1528): "Seek the word of God in all things; and without the word of God do nothing, though it appear ever so glorious. Whatsoever is done without the word of God, that count idolatry."[38]

All aspects of William Tyndale's running debate with the

spokesmen for medieval orthodoxy grew out of his inflexible adherence to *sola scriptura*. "The firm conviction that only in scripture can God's revelation for man be found, is . . . the presupposition of everything," Tyndale says. Since the Bible is the sole repository of direct special revelation, of necessity, everything requisite to man's salvation has been written in the Scripture.[40]

Like Robert Barnes, William Tyndale had a high regard for some of the Fathers of the ancient Church, especially St. Augustine, whom he called the "best, or one of the best, that ever wrote upon the scripture."[41] However, Tyndale insisted that the writings of Augustine and of all other patristic authors be subjected to continual scrutiny in the light of Scripture. Tyndale was confident that he had found in some of Augustine's works Platonic ideas which were incompatible with genuine Christianity. Tyndale likewise argued that it was on the basis of Biblical authority alone that "we damn some of Origen's works, and allow some. . . . The scripture (being) the trial of all doctrine and the right touchstone."[42] For those Fathers he deemed unsound, Tyndale had nothing but scorn.

> Get thee to God's word, and thereby try all doctrine, and against that receive nothing; . . . And when they (the papists) cry "Fathers, Fathers," remember that it were the fathers that blinded and robbed the whole world, and brought us into this captivity, wherein they enforce to keep us still.[43]

By taking the position that God's saving revelation is confined to the Bible, Tyndale was making a frontal assault upon the belief that revelation is both Scriptural and institutional; that is, the same God who spoke through the Biblical authors continues to speak through the organized Church expressing itself in the decrees of popes and councils. Furthermore, the Roman Church held that its claim to be the channel of continuing revelation was verified by divine interventions in the form of miracles. This was a major point of emphasis in More's argument.[44]

In his reply to More, Tyndale argues that miracles were indeed channels of revelation but that divine revelation ceased with the completion of the New Testament, and, therefore, miracles ceased concurrently. He sternly rebuked More by saying, "where we can confound your false doctrine with authentic and manifest scripture, there we need to do no miracle."[45] This was an argument with which Robert Barnes was in agreement.[46]

Yet the reformers did not categorically deny the validity of all miracles claimed by the papists. Tyndale rather argued that all claims to the miraculous must be judged by Scripture, and that when they were, many would be found to be bogus. He specifically accused the pope of advertising false miracles in order to deceive Christian people.[47] Nevertheless, the reformers did admit that supernatural events of religious significance occasionally did occur, but they assigned them to demonic rather than divine influence. Luther said, "Satan, in order to destroy faith, did many signs through visitations from saints, apparitions of spirits, and the like."[48] Tyndale quite bluntly ascribed the miracles put forth by the papists to the work of Satan, who used them to distract men from the written Word of God.[49] Like Luther, Barnes and all the major reformers, Tyndale insisted that real Christian faith is based upon the Word, not upon miracles.[50]

Because he believed so fervently in the authority of Scripture, William Tyndale made the project of producing a readable and accurate English translation of the Bible the goal of his life. He was convinced that the priests and prelates of England were the greatest hindrances to the spiritual well-being of the nation. To More he complained:

> Your church does not teach men to know the scripture, but hides it in the Latin from the common people; and from them that understand Latin they hide the true sense with a thousand false glosses.[51]

To combat the prevailing ignorance, Tyndale said he would give the laity "the scripture . . . plainly laid before their eyes in their mother tongue."[52] He believed that only by this means could the people of England be freed from the legalism of medieval Catholicism for the enjoyment of genuine Christian liberty.[53]

When Tyndale's New Testament first appeared (1526), his opponents subjected it to an exhaustive critical examination and then declared it to be full of error and heresy.[54] As one would expect, one of the most vituperative critics was Thomas More.[55] This is not to suggest, however, that More opposed the publication of an English Bible *per se*. In Erasmian fashion, he actually favored making the Scriptures available in the vernacular, but he held that such translations and their use should be regulated by episcopal supervision.[56]

As indicated above,[57] the king, More and the hierarchy could not stop the circulation and reading of Tyndale's English version, and the crown finally issued a license for the distribution of the English Bible in the version of Myles Coverdale.

Before considering the exegetical principles which guided Tyndale to his expositions of the Bible, there is the matter of the canon of Scripture, which was a major concern for Luther and, for a brief time, a problem also for Robert Barnes.

Tyndale composed prologues to every book of the New Testament except the Acts of the Apostles and St. John's Revelation.[58] Why he did not try to introduce the readers of his New Testament to these particular books is difficult to know, for he often quoted from them in support of his arguments. The present writer has found nothing in the published works of Tyndale to suggest that the reformer entertained any serious doubts about the canonicity of any of the twenty-seven books traditionally regarded as comprising the New Testament.

One may at first be confused by the undocumented remark of Professor E. G. Rupp, "There are, on careful examination, hardly any points where disagreement between Tyndale and Luther can be found, *even in the matter of James,*"[59] which is disputed by J. F. Mozley, Tyndale's biographer, who is of the firm opinion that Tyndale's view of the New Testament canon was precisely one of the most significant features that distinguished him from Luther.[60] Perhaps Professor Rupp considers Luther's practical use of James' Epistle as a source of authoritive quotations and sermon texts to be of more significance than his few disparaging remarks about it.

In his prologue to the Epistle of James, Tyndale recited some of the objections to accepting James as Scripture and then rejected every one of them, concluding, "I think it should rightly be taken for holy scripture."[61]

Except for his landmark work as a translator of the English Bible, William Tyndale made his greatest impact on Reformation thought in the area of Scripture exposition. Here, as has been incisively observed, "Tyndale is entirely to be reverenced by all Englishmen, as the founder of all rational Scriptural interpretation in England."[62] Viewing the previous work of John Colet, one might hesitate to cite Tyndale as the "founder" of rational exegesis, but no one can deny that he was the foremost exponent of thorough hermeneutical scholarship in the early English Reformation.

William Tyndale approached the exegetical task with two commanding presuppositions: 1) the Bible constitutes the only saving revelation from God, and 2) personal faith in Christ as one's only Savior is prerequisite to the proper understanding of the sacred text. The Scripture is clear to those who read it in faith, so the believing reader is spiritually equipped to use the Bible as his guide in discerning truth and falsehood.[63]

According to Tyndale, faith sees Christ as the keystone of the Bible.

> All doctrine that builds . . . upon Christ to put your
> trust and confidence in his blood, is of God, and
> true doctrine; and all doctrine that withdraws
> your hope and trust from Christ is of the devil, and
> the doctrine of antichrist. Examine the Roman
> bishop by this rule.[64]

To his credit, Tyndale also asked his readers to apply the above test to his own treatises, expressing the confidence that the readers would find them Christ-centered, and, therefore, Scripturally sound.[65]

Since it appears that both Barnes and Tyndale derived the Christocentricity of their Bible interpretation from Luther, it is appropriate at this point to allow their German tutor to set forth the essence of this exegetical principle. For Luther, Christ is the center of Scripture because he is the living Word of God who brings forgiveness of sin through the Gospel. The Scripture is God's Word speaking through Law and Gospel, and the proper distinction between these two vehicles of revelation is utterly indispensable for a correct understanding of the Bible. Luther summarized his view in his 1535 exposition of Paul's Epistle to the Galatians.

> It is sufficiently evident what the distinction is between the Law and the Gospel. The Law never brings the Holy Spirit; therefore it does not justify. because it only teaches what we ought to do. But the Gospel does bring the Holy Spirit, because it teaches what we ought to receive. Therefore the Law and the Gospel are two altogether contrary doctrines. Accordingly, to put righteousness into the Law is simply to conflict with the Gospel. For the Law is a taskmaster; it demands that we work and that we give. In short, it wants to have something from us. The Gospel, on the contrary, does not demand; it grants freely; it commands us to hold out our hands and to receive what is being offered. Now demanding and granting, receiving and offering, are exact opposites and cannot exist together. . . . Therefore, if the Gospel is a gift and offers a gift, it does not demand anything. On the other hand, the Law does not grant anything; it makes demands on us, and impossible ones at that.[66]

Luther found Law and Gospel side-by-side throughout the Bible, since both testaments abound with demands for human works, which belong in the category of Law, but, also, with promises of the free forgiveness of sin, which are expressions of the Gospel. Both Law and Gospel are God's

Word. The Law condemns the sinner, and the Gospel gives forgiveness through Christ. To Luther, the Law-Gospel motif is the principle which gives unity to the Scriptures.

Tyndale's first effort at publishing his doctrinal views appeared in a prologue which he composed for the first edition of his English New Testament. It was subsequently reissued in a slightly modified version under the title *A Pathway into the Holy Scripture* (1525). Here Master Tyndale quickly showed his subscription to the Lutheran Law-Gospel construct. Tyndale held that Law and Gospel are found together throughout the Bible, but that the Old Testament was primarily a book of Law and the New Testament a book of Gospel. Since man cannot possibly fulfill all the requirements of the Law, he must turn to the Gospel with its promises of mercy in Christ.[67] In his later years, Tyndale diverged from Luther regarding the role of divine Law in the life of a Christian,[68] but he never abandoned the essential Lutheran overview of the Bible from the Law-Gospel perspective.

Recognizing that Tyndale regarded faith in Christ as the necessary spiritual qualification, and comprehension of the Law-Gospel motif as the intellectual prerequisite, we may next inquire about the procedural methods of his Biblical exegesis.

Robert Barnes' insistence upon making the Bible its own primary interpreter by comparing Scripture with Scripture was also a key exegetical principle for William Tyndale. Tyndale was especially opposed to the practice of citing individual verses from the Bible as proof-texts in support of disputed doctrinal positions. He emphasized the constant need of first considering the context from which a given Scripture portion is taken. Surely, he would have subscribed to the current hermeneutical proverb: "A text out of context is but a pretext." Tyndale stated this matter succinctly. "One scripture will help to declare another. And the circumstances, that is to say, the places that go before and after, will give light unto the middle text."[69]

Tyndale elaborated on the need for a thorough searching of the Scriptures to ascertain the overall sense of the Bible on any given doctrine. He believed that when the Apostle Peter wrote, "no prophecy in the Scripture has any private interpretation" (2 Peter 1:20), he was admonishing his readers to consider the whole context and tenor of Scripture in arriving at an understanding of the Christological prophecies of the Old Testament.[70]

Both Tyndale and Barnes held that their exegesis would lead to the restoration of the original beliefs and practices of the Christian Church. As Barnes put it,

> If man had stuck to the open scriptures of God and to the practice of Christ's holy church, . . . it would not have been necessary for me to have taken these pains and labors in this cause.[71]

As Barnes and Tyndale saw it, to the degree that the medieval Church deviated from the Scriptures, it deviated from the divine pattern for ecclesiastical belief and practice. The medieval ecclesiastical structure had ceased to be the Church, Biblically defined. Medieval exegetes thus were guilty of going contrary to "open texts, and the general articles of the faith, and the whole course of the Scripture and contrary to the living and practicing of Christ and the Apostles and holy prophets."[72]

Tyndale found the greatest flaw in medieval Biblical interpretation in its preoccupation with allegorical, rather than literal-historical exegesis. A major portion of *The Obedience of a Christian Man* (1528) is concerned with refuting the medieval practice of seeking the so called "four senses of the Scripture." With considerably more thoroughness and exactitude than Barnes, Tyndale assailed the hermeneutics of the schoolmen. His arguments were based upon the dogmatic assertion that "the scripture has but one sense, which is the literal sense."[73] The failure to realize this may be traced back at least to Origen (d. 254) and the Alexandrian school of thinkers who tried to synthesize revealed Christian truth and speculative Greek philosophy. Tyndale saw the medieval scholastics as the exegetical heirs of Origen and the pervasiveness of their influence as a major cause of the prevalent spiritual decadence and Biblical ignorance.[74]

Of course, Tyndale recognized that the Bible sometimes uses metaphors, proverbs, and even allegories, but he insisted that the real meaning and application of these figures is to be sought by rigorous grammatical-historical exegesis and not by flight of fancy into the ethereal realms of speculation. Faithful adherence to this method of exegesis will yield the actual (literal) sense of even allegorical passages.[75] This is the procedure which he urged upon the readers of his prologues to the books of the Bible.

> Cleave unto the text and plain story, and endeavour ... to search out the meaning of all that is described therein, and the true sense ... of the scripture; ... and beware of subtle allegories.[76]

Tyndale was confident that the wide reading of the Scriptures in the English language would expose the sophistries of scholastic exegesis. He believed that it was for this reason that the clergy tended to oppose a vernacular translation.[77]

Just as Tyndale found faith in Christ essential to the proper approach to the Bible, he regarded the supernatural guidance of the Holy Spirit as the concomitant requirement.

Although Robert Barnes did not write on this aspect of hermeneutics, Tyndale made it a major portion of his discourses on the proper way to read and use the Scriptures.

In his debate with Sir Thomas More, William Tyndale claimed that, in the final analysis, it is the internal witness of the Holy Spirit which draws men to believe the Bible, and demonic influence which deters them. "The Spirit of God teaches his children to believe; and the devil blinds his children, and keeps them in unbelief."[78] He saw the Bible as the instrument employed by the Holy Spirit to enlighten men with divine truth. This operation of the Spirit is personal and direct, rather than institutional and indirect. Here was the heart of his controversy with More. "According to More, the Holy Spirit brings man to belief in the Church, according to Tyndale to belief in the scripture."[79] More would not deny that the same Spirit who inspired the writers of Holy Writ guided men into the correct understanding of its message. However, Sir Thomas held that the Spirit gave that guidance to the Church, which, in turn, was the Spirit's vehicle for the enlightenment of the faithful.[80] With both disputants claiming possession of the Holy Spirit, the ultimate theological deadlock had been reached.

Because the theologians of the established Church had built the scholastic system on a Greek philosophical foundation, Tyndale concluded that the dispute over authority was ultimately a contest between the Spirit of God and the pagan spirit of Aristotle.[81] Unfortunately, Tyndale did not adequately distinguish between medieval scholasticism and renaissance Catholic humanism. Therefore, he somewhat unjustly dismissed Thomas More as a scholastic.[82]

On the question of authority, Robert Barnes and William Tyndale were united in their subscription to *sola scriptura* and opposition to traditions which ran contrary to Biblical revelation. Both reformers were unsparing in their attacks upon the exegetical practices of medieval scholasticism. Barnes and Tyndale were agreed that the clergy were the major obstacles preventing the authorization of the English Bible, so these reformers spoke out vociferously against clericalism. Barnes wrote polemic with the fervor of a tractarian. Tyndale wrote from that perspective too, but more often from the standpoint of an exegetical theologian. Like Luther, Barnes and Tyndale had no affinity for spiritualism. They were men of the Book. The lives and works of these reformer-martyrs support the conclusion: 'In the long run, the supreme fact in the reformation under Henry VIII was a religious fact, the making and opening of its Bible to the English nation.''[83]

CHAPTER 4

# THE QUESTIONS OF GOD AND MAN

## THE NATURE OF GOD

The reformers' doctrine of God contained nothing novel or extraordinary. Like Luther, Barnes and Tyndale held to the traditional concept of God as formalized in such ecumenical statements of the ancient Church as the Apostles' Creed and the Nicene Creed. The reformers would insist, however, that it was the teaching of Scripture rather than any conciliar decision which constituted the basis for their beliefs. Lack of originality was the necessary consequence of the reformers' objective. They sought for nothing new, but rather wanted to restore the doctrines of primitive Christianity to the primacy they once enjoyed.

In 1538, Luther published *The Three Symbols or Creeds of the Christian Faith,* a German translation of the Apostles' Creed, the Athanasian Creed, and the *Te Deum Laudamus* together with his own expository comments. He said that his purpose in doing this was "that I may again bear witness that I hold to the real Christian Church, which up until now has preserved these symbols or creeds, and not to that false . . . church [Rome] which is indeed the worst enemy of the real church."[1] The whole tenor of the writings of Barnes and Tyndale shows that they shared Luther's desire to demonstrate the historical continuity between their theology and the catholic orthodoxy of the ancient Church. It was for this reason that the reformers made short shrift of the philosophical-theological productions of the medieval scholastics.

Second only to their disavowal of medieval doctrinal accretions was the reformers' disdain for the theological novelties advanced by some of the radical Anabaptist and spiritualist movements. As already noted,[2] Robert Barnes served on a royal commission directed to combat Anabaptism. By dissociating themselves from the radical wing of the Reformation, the early Protestants were trying to allay the suspicion that they favored political and social revolution as advocated by some sects on the Continent. Later in the sixteenth century, when the anti-trinitarianism of Servetus and Socinus had begun to gain a following in England, the reformers also emphatically rejected the sectaries' doctrine of God.

Although the reformers' doctrine of God was deliberately non-innovative, they chose to emphasize attributes of the Deity, which, though officially endorsed by the Church since antiquity, had not been in the center of focus among theologians for centuries. One such attribute was the incorporeality of God. The spiritual essence of the divine Character was never seriously questioned by either Catholic apologists or Protestant polemicists, but the implications of this doctrine became the occasion for a protracted conflict between them. The controversy revolved around the question of whether, or to what extent, material representations of Christ and the saints may be used in Christian devotion. Both Barnes and Tyndale addressed themselves to this question energetically. The position which they took was not totally in harmony with that of Martin Luther.

After delivering his address to the Diet of Worms (1521), Luther lived in hiding for eleven months in the Wartburg Castle, a property of Frederick, Elector of Saxony. During

his absence from Wittenberg, Luther's colleague Andreas
Karlstadt became the leader of a movement which was bent
upon the destruction of all religious forms traditionally as-

ABOVE: Frederick the Wise, Elector of Saxony   BELOW: citizens of
16th-Century Europe (from an engraving by Albrecht Duerer)

sociated with the Roman mode of worship. Karlstadt and his followers particularly despised the presence of images in the churches. When Luther learned of the actual destruction of such figures, he rebuked the iconoclasts in general and Karlstadt in particular. In a treatise of 1525, entitled *Against the Heavenly Prophets in the Matter of Images and Sacraments,* he composed his objections to a number of radical practices in which Karlstadt had engaged. In the discourse Luther made it clear that he believed that Christians could use religious images without becoming involved in idolatry.[3]

Luther expressed himself on the matter of images many times, sometimes even indicating that their proper use could actually enhance Christian worship.

> I have always condemned and criticized the misuse of religious pictures and the false confidence placed in them and all the rest. But whatever is no misuse . . . I have always permitted and urged the use of for beneficial and edifying results.[4]

Luther interpreted the divine commandment against making "graven images" (Exodus 20:4) as merely forbidding the idolatrous worship of images, but when figures of Christ and the saints were used only as visible reminders of spiritual realities Luther had no objection. To the present, Lutheran sanctuaries are often adorned with a crucifix and replicas of Biblical figures.

Whatever spiritual profit Luther may have felt could be derived from the proper use of images notwithstanding, Barnes and Tyndale objected to them strenuously.

Dr. Barnes categorically rejected the religious use of images in a treatise which bore the title *That it is against the holy Scripture to honour Images and to pray to Saints.*[5]

Barnes' tirade against images begins by accusing the papists of maintaining and promoting a very inadequate understanding of the omnipotence and mercy of God. This lack of understanding he felt was responsible for the outright worship of images so widespread across Christendom. Moreover, to pray before images was to insult Jesus Christ, the only real mediator between God and man. Barnes supported his argument by alluding to the periodic outbreaks of idolatry among the Israelites of the Old Testament.[6]

The medieval Church made a distinction between the worship and the veneration of images, but to Barnes such distinctions were inexcusable sophistry. He fulminated against those who "trifle with God's holy word . . . when they think to avoid it [idolatry] with a damnable distinction."[7]

Not only did Robert Barnes denounce the religious use of images, but he also attributed the worst of motives to those who encouraged it. In language which Luther might have used in a different context, Barnes wrote against the papists.

> Because you are hypocrites and insatiable belly
> gods, you care not (so you may deceive the simple
> people and lead them with blind shadows, thereby
> to fill your offering boxes and chests to maintain
> your insatiable appetites) how the honour of God
> is served, or how your poor brethren's conscience
> is deceived.[8]

Barnes ridiculed all efforts at representing Biblical figures in picture or statue because no one knows their real likeness anyway. He was impressed that some contemporary depictions of the mother of Jesus looked "a great deal more like unto a harlot, than to a pure and a blessed meek virgin."[9]

Often, the defenders of image veneration tried to answer the reformers' charges by advertising the miracles which reportedly occurred at some of the shrines. Barnes curtly rebutted that argument by asserting that the miracles were really "illustrations of the devil, invented by your own imaginations."[10]

The strength of Barnes' arguments against the use of images was appreciably enhanced by his familiarity with the patristic authors. In this case, he appealed to the works of Jerome and Augustine, where he found their disapproval of rendering either worship or honor to images. Indeed, Barnes was able to show that the scorn with which some of the Fathers renounced images actually exceeded the severity of his own scathing criticisms.[11]

Robert Barnes' opposition to the veneration of images was mainly based on his realistic observation that the practice had become so deeply involved in superstition that it was impossible to regard it as anything but idolatry. He also had a deeper reason for his opposition. Barnes cited the Biblical passage concerning the creation of man which says that *he* was made in the "image of God" (Genesis 1:27). Although he did not offer a detailed interpretation of the passage at this point, Barnes admonished his readers to recognize "there is no other true image but man."[12] If the prelates of England wish to honor the image of God, let them devise ways to aid suffering men, for "this image dies in the streets before your doors from hunger and cold."[13] Barnes bluntly and boldly called on the practioners of image veneration to convert their wooden idols into fuel to warm the homes of their nation's poor.

Because the doctrine of the incorporeality of God was also a concern William Tyndale, he became involved in the debate over images, too. A significant portion of his reply to

Thomas More deals with the proper manner in which God is to be worshiped, and, in this connection, they debated the subject of images.

More followed the traditional scheme of distinguishing between worship and honor (veneration) where the religious use of images was concerned. Like Barnes, Tyndale felt that any such distinction was only nominal when evaluated in the light of contemporary devotional practices.[14] Nevertheless, Tyndale quite readily admitted that it was *possible* to use images in a non-idolatrous way. To do so requires that the Christian render neither worship nor honor to images, but that he use them solely as reminders of Christ and the saints of the past. "If I make an image of Christ, or of anything that Christ has done for me, in a memory, it is good, and not evil, until it is abused."[15] Indeed, Tyndale held that this was the original intention when images were introduced in the ancient Church.

While William Tyndale believed that it was theoretically possible for man in the sixteenth century to use images properly, he felt that the prevalence of superstition stemming from ignorance of the Scripture made this possibility very unlikely. He laid the blame for this condition upon the clergy.

> How is it possible that the people can worship images, relics, ceremonies, and sacraments except superstitiously; so long as they know not the true meaning, neither will the prelates allow any man to tell them; yes, and the very meaning of some, and the right use, no man can tell?[16]

Tyndale agreed with Barnes that the spiritual part of human nature made man the real "image of God" on earth. Furthermore, he argued that all other creatures and objects were made to serve man. Since images are made by man, they must be his inferiors. To worship them is to earn damnation. "Man is lord over them, and they created to serve him, . . . and not he to serve them."[17]

The encouragement which the priesthood generally gave to superstitious religious practices was surely a major factor which provoked the unrelenting anticlericalism with which Tyndale's writings are imbued. The lavish sums of money spent by the clergy to pay for the pageantry associated with noted shrines offended Tyndale greatly. Like Barnes, he had an element of social consciousness in his thinking, which cried out against this waste. Tyndale rebuked the priests for adorning their shrines while "the poor are despised and uncared for."[18]

In the controversy over images then, the thinking of Tyndale placed him in a position somewhere between Martin Luther and Robert Barnes. Where Luther held the non-idolatrous use of images to be a thing indifferent — an option for the Christian — and Barnes abominated the practice altogether, Tyndale allowed for the possibility of their proper use but discouraged the practice because of the scope of superstition current in his day.

Another of the divine attributes which the reformers felt obliged to expound and to defend was the total sovereignty of God. The details of their apology need not concern us at this point, but it is fitting to show how their concept of divine sovereignty brought them into conflict with the papists, again over the matter of proper worship.

Because they believed that God is totally sovereign, the reformers had no place in their theology for the worship of anyone other than God. Their insistence upon God's exclusive right to receive worship ran directly contrary to the vast cult of praying to the saints, a practice with hundreds of years of tradition behind it.

The medieval Church never actually authorized the adoration of its canonized saints. It rather portrayed the saints as worthy mediators who could intercede with God for those who petitioned them in prayer. In this, as in the case of images, a fine line of distinction separated "worship" from "veneration."

In the first few years following his espousal of justification by faith alone, Luther continued the monastic custom of invoking the intercession of the canonized departed. In 1520, however, in his treatise *On the Babylonian Captivity of the Church,* he denounced the "perverse worship of the saints."[19] Thereafter, he often attacked the whole medieval cult revolving around prayer to the saints. In a polemical treatise of 1541, Luther challenged his opponents,

> Who has commanded you to set up this new idolatry of worshiping the saints, canonizing them, and appointing fast days on which to honor them, just as if they were God himself, so that men rely on . . . their merit more than in Christ himself, his blood and his merit?[20]

Once they had broken with Rome, Robert Barnes and William Tyndale followed Luther's lead in repudiating the cult of the saints. They saw that the actual worship of the saints was a prominent feature of popular piety, so they lashed out against it as dishonoring the sovereign God.

Barnes launched a furious assault on the concept of the saints' mediatorship. "There cannot be a thing invented by the craft of the devil that may be a greater blasphemy or more derogation to Christ and his blessed blood than this is."[21] He held this was so because Scripture designates

Christ as the "one mediator between God and man" (1 Timothy 2:5). Barnes argued that the saints cannot qualify as mediators with God because they are mere men, sinful men at that. Therefore, they need the mediatorship of Christ just as much as any other men. Moreover, Barnes urged his readers to follow the example of the "saints" who appear on the pages of the Bible. They prayed only to God.[22]

Although his essay against venerating images and praying to saints is rather typical of the invective style in which he wrote, it does contain an occasional passage which shows that Robert Barnes was capable of tenderness. In the midst of this treatise Barnes momentarily suspended the attack against his theological opponents to show deep personal concern for the spiritual welfare of his readers.

> Dear Brethren, if you would be Christ's make him only your mediator and your intercessor to the Father of heaven, and all things you desire, desire them in his name only. Make him first your friend and then you have all saints on your side.[23]

Sir Thomas More, in his polemics against the reformers, proposed to defend almost every ecclesiastical practice which they condemned. Therefore, he sought to justify prayers to the saints, as well as the veneration of images. He argued against Tyndale that prayer to the saints actually honors God. Tyndale dogmatically replied, "if our faith in God were greater than our fervent devotion to saints, we should pray to no saints at all, seeing we have promises of all things in our Savior Jesus, and in the saints none at all."[24] Tyndale further reasoned that when saints of Bible days were alive they did not ask men to trust in their powers, so why should men regard them as potent intercessors after they were dead?[25] Likewise, Tyndale wanted More to explain why the vast array of canonized persons had no miracles attributed to them until they were dead?[26]

Tyndale insisted that the real saints in heaven trusted solely in Christ, and, therefore, they would abhor prayers directed to them from people on earth.[27] "The merits of saints did not save themselves, but [they] were saved by Christ's merits only."[28]

ABOVE: Sir Thomas More   BELOW: the More family as portrayed in Holbein's famous pen-and-ink drawing.

William Tyndale pointedly and repeatedly denounced the practice of praying to the saints, because he could find no Scriptural warrant for it. Instead, he found that the cult of the saints was incompatible with the Biblical doctrine of God as the only absolute sovereign entitled to the undivided adoration of his subjects. Tyndale held that the only way to honor the saints without detracting from the glory of God and denying the mediatorship of Christ is to believe the doctrine which the saints taught and to follow their example of Christ-likeness.[29]

Since More and the reformers approached these controversies with irreconcilable presuppositions, of necessity they reached mutually exclusive conclusions. Even when they debated the meaning of selected texts of Scripture there was no real possibility of agreement. More saw the Church as the judge of Scripture, and the reformers insisted that the Church had been judged by the Scripture and found wanting.

In Reformation theology, the God who is over all has revealed himself as a tri-unity, that is, one deity manifesting himself in three fully divine persons — Father, Son, and Holy Spirit. In taking this unequivocally trinitarian position, the reformers placed themselves in the mainstream of orthodoxy flowing from the ancient Church. Therefore there could be no serious controversy between them and the Roman apologists with regard to the tri-personal nature of God. When Robert Barnes wrote, "Our Master Christ . . . was not only of God, but also God himself, and all that he did was done by the counsel of the whole Trinity,"[30] no Catholic theologian would take exception. Nor could they quarrel with Luther when he declared, "There is one God and three persons, God the Father, God the Son, and God the Holy Spirit; in one and the same substance, majesty, power, work, and honor; who created the heavens and the earth."[31]

The Protestant reformers, nevertheless, drew implications from their trinitarianism, which they occasionally employed in their debates with spokesmen of the established Church. They felt that the doctrine of the Trinity had particular relevance to the dispute about the intercession of the saints. It is precisely because he is both God and man that Christ is the only effectual mediator with the Father. To resort to other mediators is to derogate from the deity of Christ. Barnes cited St. John Chrysostom (d. 407) on this point. "They that make other mediators but Christ only mistrust Christ and believe that he is not omnipotent God nor merciful Lord, and, therefore, they fly unto this saint and unto that saint, trusting to find more mercy at their hands than they could at Christ's."[32]

Fundamental to an understanding of the reformers' doctrine of God is their epistemology. In this, as in their discussions of the Trinity, the Protestant theologians scrupulously avoided speculation and rationalization. It was the common conception among them that God may be known solely because of his self-disclosure.

Martin Luther made the doctrine of the knowledge of God a recurrent theme in his writings, and his position on this question was generally shared by the major English reformers. Robert Barnes did not address himself to this question except as it related to his concept of *sola scriptura,* and William Tyndale likewise treated it only incidentally. Still, the doctrine of the knowledge of God was so fundamental in Reformation thought that the Evangelical position should be outlined, even though Luther, rather than Barnes or Tyndale, was the spokesman.

The reformers acknowledged that nature itself was one

instrument of the divine self-disclosure. The witness of nature to the reality of God's existence is inescapable, so men everywhere acknowledge a supernatural being or beings, as the religions of the world testify. The fall of the human race in Adam and Eve, however, has impaired man's powers of spiritual perception so that he does not apprehend the true God in nature but rather distorts the natural revelation. The worship of nature itself, personified and often idolized, is the result. Consequently, man cannot obtain a saving knowledge of God merely from the revelation in nature.[33]

Although man cannot attain to the knowledge of God as savior through the revelation of nature, man's faculty of reason does equip him to grasp something of the divine moral requirements, and thus some men arrive at what Luther called a "legal knowledge" of God. This type of knowledge then must be contrasted with the true knowledge which leads to salvation.

> There are two kinds of knowledge of God: the one is the knowledge of the Law; the other is the knowledge of the Gospel. For God issued the Law and the Gospel that he might be known through them. Reason is familiar with the knowledge of God which is based on the Law, . . . for from the Law it saw the difference between right and wrong. The Law is also inscribed in our hearts, as St. Paul testifies to the Romans (Romans 2:15). . . . It still remains true that all rational beings of themselves can determine that it is wrong to disobey father and mother and the government, to murder, commit adultery, steal, curse, and blaspheme. Therefore transgressors of the law, whoremongers, murderers, thieves, and similar rascals

. . . had to admit their wrongdoing in court; for their own conscience tells them that it is not right for one man to kill another. They have the content of the Law of God . . . written in their hearts by nature. . . .

Reason can arrive at a "legal knowledge" of God. It is conversant with God's Commandments and can distinguish between right and wrong. The philosophers, too, had this knowledge of God. But the knowledge of God derived from the Law is not the true knowledge of him, whether it be the Law of Moses or the Law instilled into our hearts.[34]

There is a twofold knowledge of God: the general and the particular. All men have the general knowledge, namely, that God is, . . . but what God thinks of us, what he wants to give and to do to deliver us from sin and death and to save us — which is the particular and true knowledge of God — this men do not know. . . . So it is that men know naturally that there is a God, but they do not know what he wants and what he does not want. . . . Now what good does it do you to know that God exists if you do not know what his will is toward you?[35]

According to Luther, it is only through the special revelation — the Word of God — that man may arrive at the proper knowledge of God. This is the "knowledge of the Gospel," and it alone is the knowledge which brings salvation.[36]

Although, as indicated, Barnes and Tyndale did not expound on the knowledge of God with the depth and frequency of Luther, there is an illuminating passage in the

*Obedience of a Christian Man* which clearly shows Tyndale's concurrence with Luther's epistemology.

> Man's wisdom is plain idolatry: neither is there any other idolatry than to imagine of God after man's wisdom. God is not man's imagination; but only that which he says of himself. God is nothing but his law and his promises; that is to say, that which he bids you to do, and that which he bids you believe and hope. God is but his word, . . . and to imagine any other thing of God than that, is damnable idolatry.[37]

The God of Luther, Barnes, and Tyndale and all the Evangelical reformers was the triune, sovereign, and self-revealing Spirit who has made himself savingly known in Jesus Christ through the Gospel. Their belief that the true knowledge of God comes only to those who believe the Gospel made these reformers zealots for the translation and circulation of the Scripture in the language of the people.

## THE NATURE OF MAN

The late Professor Conyers Read once remarked that the Renaissance

> in its essence was a changed attitude of mind towards man and his environment, substituting for the medieval conception of man as a miserable sinner striving against the world and the flesh, man as an interesting and beautiful creature in a beautiful and interesting world.[38]

As a generalization, this observation is quite valid, but, as with all generalizations, liable to some qualifications. Apart from the advent of humanist linguistic-textual scholarship and the invention of the printing press, it is unlikely that a Protestant Reformation could have taken place in the sixteenth century. All the major reformers in some measure employed the tools of humanist learning in the cause of restoring the Church in the Biblical mold. Those same reformers, however, rejected emphatically the humanist anthropology, which saw man as inherently good, and, therefore, potentially capable of the highest moral, ethical, and spiritual attainments. The humanist idea that proper tutorial guidance could lead man to moral and ethical maturity was a concept the reformers found abhorrent because, in their view, it minimized the corrupting effects of sin. The reformers saw man as a sinner whose entire nature had been contaminated so that he was inherently powerless to achieve spiritual good.

Although the reformers rejected the doctrine of man's innate goodness, they did not merely perpetuate the anthropology of the medieval Church. On the contrary, the doctrine of man became one of the most hotly debated issues between Romanists and reformers. Indeed, every controversy between them had some connection with this issue. Whereas the humanist view conflicted with that of the medieval Church, the Protestant view conflicted with both.

Because he was the only creature said to have been made in the "image of God," the reformers regarded man as the crown of the creation — the highest expression of the deity's genius. Luther said that the image of God "dignifies the nature of man in . . . a glorious manner and distinguishes it from all other creatures."[39] Consequently, man, as he came fresh from the hand of his Creator, had "an enlightened reason, a true knowledge of God, and a most sincere desire to love God and his neighbor."[40] The divine image in man, however, was obscured and corrupted when Adam and Eve fell into sin. The consequences of that corruption became a subject of furious and protracted debate, which occupied some of the finest minds of the sixteenth century.

Controversy about the effects of "original sin," as Adam's first transgression was called, had been a recurrent problem for the Church since ancient times. Perhaps the most famous theologians who had debated this matter were Augustine (d. 430) and Pelagius (d. 420), a monk from the British Isles. Pelagius argued that since man is commanded by God to keep the divine law, this presupposes his ability to keep that law. In the Pelagian view, original sin had no great effect upon Adam's posterity. Human nature is basically good despite the fall, and it sins only through following bad example. The continual following of bad example makes sin habitual, but human nature is not depraved. Pelagius admitted man's need for divine grace, but held that its role was "an enlightenment of man's reason, enabling him to see the will of God so that man of his own powers can choose and act accordingly."[41]

The views of Pelagius encountered opposition early in the fifth century, and Augustine, Bishop of Hippo, became his principal adversary. On the basis of Biblical exegesis, Augustine taught that all mankind was implicated in Adam's fall and that God imputed Adam's guilt to his posterity. This is original sin, and its consequence is that all men are born with a nature inclined toward evil. Ensnared by the desires of his sinful flesh, man willingly pursues evil. Indeed, he cannot do otherwise because he is lacking in the desire to please God. Depraved by nature, man possesses neither the will nor the ability to change his condition. His only hope is in divine grace.[42]

After much debate, the Augustinian position prevailed,

and Pelagianism was declared heretical at the Council of Ephesus (431).

Augustine's view of sin and grace, nevertheless, did not win universal acceptance. A Semi-Pelagian school eventually arose to charge Augustine with fatalism. Semi-Pelagians argued that the depravity due to original sin was real, but that it did not extend to the loss of free will, as Augustine had taught. This attack on the Augustinian anthropology was repelled by the Synod of Orange, in 529. Officially, therefore, the Augustinian position had triumphed. Orange, however, denied that the grace of salvation is irresistible, as Augustine had taught. Therefore it was a somewhat modified Augustinianism which was endorsed at Orange.

Through the Middle Ages, the concept of human merit in salvation steadily gained acceptance, and Augustine's theology was eclipsed. Semi-Pelagianism revived and was finally confronted by a revived Augustinianism in the work of Luther and Calvin.

By the time that Luther began his career as a theologian, Semi-Pelagianism had made deep inroads among the scholastic theologians. Two particularly notable scholastic Semi-Pelagians were William of Occam (d. 1349), an English Franciscan, and Gabriel Biel (d. 1495), a professor at Tuebingen. Early in his teaching career, Luther found the beliefs of Occam and Biel on sin and grace in error. Therefore he broke with the prevailing scholastic theology.[43] Luther returned to the Augustinian doctrine of man, and Barnes and Tyndale eventually followed him.

Robert Barnes outlined his anthropology in an essay entitled *Free will of man, after the fall of Adam of hys naturall strength, can doe nothyng but sinne beefore God.*[44] His argument was that man's depravity is so extensive that he can never entertain a truly godly desire apart from divine grace.

101

Although he may perform deeds which are judged good by human standards, they are not meritorious in God's sight. The human will is free only in "inferior and worldly things, as what power he has in eating and drinking, in sleeping and speaking, in buying and selling, and in all other natural things."[45]

In the spiritual realm Barnes concluded:

> Free will is so blind that it does not recognize sin as sin or virtue as virtue, but regards that which is evil as good because it is lost and has no true judgment. . . . Man sins by free will and sin has the victory, then free will is completely lost.[46]

The paralysis of the will in spiritual matters was for Barnes merely a reflection of natural man's spiritually dead condition. Adam's exercise of free will brought sin and death. Therefore, "St. Augustine calls it cursed free will." Evil desires originate in the heart of man, and evil deeds "are chosen by the election of the free will."[47]

Barnes' scholastic critics objected that God could not command obedience to his law if man lacked the power to comply. Barnes replied to this Pelagian argument with his typical polemical language.

> O you blind and presumptuous and damnable reason. Where have you learned . . . to inquire [for] a cause of your Maker's will? . . . He has made you without your consent, . . . may he not set laws . . . to rule you, at his pleasure, without your counsel? You are worthy of no answer. You are so presumptuous.[48]

Much of the treatise on the will is concerned with refuting objections to what his critics labeled Barnes' "Lutheranism." Basically, it was the historic Augustinian anthropology which Luther had rediscovered and conveyed to Barnes. One of the chief objections to this view of human inability was that it made a mockery of the divine commandments and called into question the essential goodness of God. To this charge Barnes affirmed the goodness of all God's precepts and concluded that man's inability was no reflection on the goodness of the Deity. Man should be content to acknowledge that it is God's "pleasure so to command." God gave the commandments to expose human evil and inability. Man should admit his condition and flee to Christ for mercy. For God "gave you these commandments for that intent, secretly declaring both your pride, and also your weakness, that you might seek and call to him for help."[49] Barnes reminded his readers that this was St. Augustine's teaching.

The leading scholastic theologians of the late Middle Ages did not espouse a consistent Pelagianism. As indicated, it was a Semi-Pelagianism which they advocated, and, in so doing, they felt that they had paid sufficient tribute to the need for divine grace in salvation. Through following Thomas Aquinas, the scholastics held that man has the free will to prepare himself for grace. This grace is then infused into man, enabling him to perform good works deserving of eternal reward in heaven.[50] This view held the allegiance of the leading English theologians at the dawn of the Reformation. It was the position espoused by Thomas More in his disputes with William Tyndale, and it was the theological standpoint from which the eloquent Bishop John Fisher accused the reformers of fatalism and making God the author of evil.

Dr. Barnes answered Bishop Fisher's accusation of fatalism by charging the latter with Pelagianism. The reformer insisted that all good intentions are provoked by grace. "Be-

fore grace, he [man] is an utter enemy of God. . . . Where-
fore, God must of his mere mercy, mollify his heart, and give
him grace to will goodness, or else he can neither do it, nor
yet desire it."[51]

The Catholic opponents of the reformers' doctrine of man
also objected that it was contradicted by many texts of
Scripture which explicitly appeal to man's will. Barnes replied that the texts in question surely are directed to man's
will, but sin has rendered his will impotent to respond ac-
ceptably. "Free will of hys owne strength can doe nothyng
but sinne beefore God" was his answer.

The scholastics were quick to see in the title of this mono-
graph terminology which could be taken to mean that man
is a mere automaton who sins of necessity. This is a rational
deduction which Barnes took pains to deny. His answer was
that man sins because he wants to. The human will naturally desires to sin, and "is not thereto constrained, but wills it
freely without compulsion."[52] God simply allows men to follow the appetites of their corrupt natures. What they do is
produced without coercion.

Although one might logically conclude that the Evangelical anthropology made God the author of evil, as his adversaries charged, Robert Barnes emphatically denied that
conclusion. He made no attempt to compose a theodicy. To
do so would have violated his own principle of *sola scriptura*.
Therefore, he simply stated his case in Scriptural terms and
ignored the philosophical problem posed by the question.
Since God is sovereign, evil is under his control, but he is not
its author.

God works good, and evil works evil, and God uses
them both as instruments. Yet he does nothing
evil, but evil is done only through the evil man,

God working by him (but not evil) as by an instrument.[53]

Those who are familiar with the Luther-Erasmus debate concerning the role of the will in salvation will recognize that Barnes was wholly committed to Luther's position. Even his choice of language gives the impression that Barnes may have been paraphrasing Luther at times. Barnes' summary of his doctrine of man could well have been written by his German mentor word-for-word. "After the fall of Adam, the pure nature of man was corrupted by sin, whereby we are all wicked and born by nature the children of wrath. . . . We are all conceived in sin."[54] Barnes and Luther stood squarely in the Augustinian tradition, and the ideas contained in Barnes' essay on free will all have close parallels in Luther's *Bondage of the Will.*[55]

While Robert Barnes stated his anthropology mainly in his attacks upon the scholastic theologians, William Tyndale, like Martin Luther, also engaged in debate with one of Europe's most renowned humanists. Luther disputed with Erasmus and Tyndale with Erasmus' disciple and close personal friend, Thomas More. As Barnes tended to paraphrase Luther, More often repeated the arguments of Erasmus.

Like all previous Christian thinkers, Tyndale believed that man, as the image of God, was created good and once enjoyed harmonious correspondence and fellowship with God. Likewise, he held that the fall of Adam disrupted that felicity, and, that all men are stained with original sin as a consequence of Adam's fall. Had he not gone beyond this point in defining his doctrine of man, Master Tyndale would have incurred the censure of neither the scholastics nor the Christian humanists.

Tyndale, however, saw the recovery of a truly Biblical anthropology as crucial to the reform of the Church. Therefore he defined his position unequivocally and reaffirmed it repeatedly. Tyndale explicitly told More that all men are "by nature made the children of sin, so that we sin naturally; and to sin is our nature."[56] In his preface to the Epistle to the Romans, Tyndale was equally clear and emphatic.

> Sin in the scripture is not . . . only that outward work committed by the body, but all the whole business, . . . of that poisonous inclination and corrupt nature, wherein he [man] was conceived and born.[57]

Because all men are by nature sinners, they have no intrinsic capacity to believe God's Word. Unbelief is the birth-condition of the entire race, and from that unbelief all other sins originate. "As faith is the mother of all goodness and of all good works; so is unbelief the ground and root of all evil and all evil works."[58]

Tyndale, then, saw natural man apart from the grace of Christ as existing in a state of spiritual bondage, which he did not hesitate to call spiritual death. To talk about the "free will" of a "dead" man, to Tyndale, was absurd.[59] To the contrary, man is insensitive to God's Word and refuses to admit his condition. The law of God should be preached to man so that he may experience a sense of his guilt and condemnation.

Believing that man by nature is spiritually dead, Tyndale denied that man could perform any meritorious works to qualify himself for the divine favor. "A man must be good, before he can do good."[60] That is, his nature must be changed before he can do genuinely good works. As Jesus taught, "every good tree brings forth good fruit; but a corrupt tree brings forth evil fruit" (Matthew 7:17).

Tyndale's exposition of Christ's Sermon on the Mount gave heavy emphasis to the belief that faith in Christ must precede good works. Even though the outward deeds may be accounted good by society, if they are not preceded by faith, they do not stem from the proper motive, and, therefore, are not accepted as truly good by God. The divine "law requires the ground of the heart, and love from the bottom thereof."[61] Unbelievers do not love God and his law, so they cannot fulfill the law by mere external conformity to its precepts.

This was largely Luther's position now reproduced for English readers. The German reformer often expressed his interpretation in virtually identical terms, as for example, "good works come from a person who has already been justified beforehand by faith, just as good fruits come from a tree which is already good beforehand by nature."[62]

Although William Tyndale did not compose a single treatise on the subject of the will as did Robert Barnes and Martin Luther, his anthropology presupposed the same opinion regarding the impotence of the will which was expressed in their writings. Tyndale's teaching on this subject may easily be gleaned from some of his most influential writings, as will become apparent presently.

In their debate, Thomas More assumed the Semi-Pelagian view of the will, which had become the hallmark of late medieval scholasticism, and Tyndale advocated the Augustinian-Lutheran position.

Tyndale categorically denied that free will could in any sense prepare man to receive divine grace. "Faith comes not of our free will; but is the gift of God, given us by grace, before there be any will in our hearts to do the law of God."[63] Rather than seek God, "free will" can only seek the satisfaction of sinful desires. Speaking of his own life before he trusted in Christ, Tyndale wrote:

> We were stone dead, and without life or power to do or consent to good. The whole nature of us was captive under the devil, and led at his will. And we were as wicked as the devil now is, . . . and we consented unto sin with soul and body, and hated the law of God.[64]

Like Barnes, Tyndale hastened to deny the charge that his view of the impotent will reduced man to a mere puppet manipulated by a capricious God. Because of his natural inclination toward evil, man does not need any compulsion in that direction. Indeed, Tyndale argued that man sins freely and willingly. "When we say that every man has his free will to do what he desires, I say, truly that men do what they desire. Notwithstanding, to follow lusts is not freedom, but captivity and bondage."[65] Consequently, the will cannot produce faith any more than a child could give birth to his father.[66]

Finally, Tyndale addressed himself to the specific accusation that the Evangelical doctrine of man, of which he was a prominent exponent, was built upon the postulate that the origin of evil is to be found in God.

Like Barnes, Tyndale dealt with the problem of evil from a strictly Biblical-theological standpoint, dismissing the philosophical issues as irreverent objections from unbelieving minds. He freely admitted that the power to do evil as well as good comes from God, but indicated that evil deeds are the consequences of man's abuse of that power. When man acts corruptly, it is due to "his blindness' fault only, and not God's: which blindness the devil has poisoned him with."[67]

Both Barnes and Tyndale were intent upon denying that God was the cause of evil. By offering only a biblical explanation, however, they could not hope to satisfy their critics. The reformers were really admitting that they did not have an answer to the question of evil, for divine revelation had never conveyed such an answer. In taking this position, Barnes and Tyndale remained faithful to their principle of *sola scriptura.* To those oriented toward the heavily philosophical theology of scholasticism, the reformers' position had to seem like an evasion.

The Protestant doctrine of man as expounded by Barnes and Tyndale reflects the revival of Augustinianism for which Luther was the pioneer spokesman. These reformers saw man as the bearer of a badly marred divine image — a sinner by nature and choice whose only hope was in the grace of Christ. God's will, ultimately, was the only defense they offered for their anthropology — which was consistent with their doctrine of God. As Luther put it, "God is he for whose will no cause or ground may be laid down as its rule and standard; for nothing is on a level with it or above it, but it is itself the rule for all things."[68]

## CHAPTER 5

# THE QUESTION OF SALVATION

## PREDESTINATION

The most noted doctrinal controversy of the Reformation era was the dispute over whether salvation is the unmerited gift of divine grace or a reward for human effort. To begin a discussion of the question at that point, however, is misleading, for underlying the entire matter is the issue of predestination. The reformers' view on this subject was the necessary consequence of their doctrine of God and man. It forms the context within which the larger question of salvation should be studied.

Believing that God is sovereign and man in bondage to sin, and on the basis of clear Scripture passages, the major Protestant reformers of the sixteenth century espoused the doctrine that God had chosen those whom he designed to save even before he created the world. Their doctrine of God and man made no allowance for contingency in the matter of salvation.[1] Following Luther, once more, Barnes and Tyndale wanted to destroy any notions of inherent righteousness, meritorious works, freedom of the will, or chance, where salvation was concerned. In taking a firm stand on predestination, they felt that they were advancing the only view of salvation which magnifies the glory of God. Luther wrote a major treatise on the subject in his *Bondage of the Will,* and Barnes and Tyndale largely followed his arguments in their writings.

There was nothing revolutionary nor historically unortho-dox about the doctrine of predestination as stated by Lu-ther, Barnes, and Tyndale. Had it appeared in an earlier epoch of Church history, it probably would have aroused much less controversy. By the sixteenth century, however, Semi-Pelagianism had achieved such a commanding influ-ence that the reformers' renewed emphasis on the Pauline-Augustinian tradition seemed like a radical innovation.

With regard to the question of predestination, there was no debate in the early English Reformation comparable to the Luther-Erasmus controversy on the Continent. There is an abundance of evidence, however, to show that Barnes and Tyndale considered acceptance of the Lutheran view on predestination as fundamental to their efforts for the restoration of Biblical Christianity. The only aspect of pre-destination which concerned them was the Bible's concept of "election," or predestination as it relates to the *salvation* of individual men.

In his essay on free will, Robert Barnes wrote mainly to rebut the Semi-Pelagian arguments of the scholastics, par-ticularly the Englishman Duns Scotus (d. 1308). The scholastics had argued that election was based upon God's foreknowledge of which men would make themselves de-serving of eternal life through good works motivated by free will. Appealing to St. Paul's Epistle to the Romans, and call-ing St. Augustine as a corroboratory witness, Barnes replied that the sovereign will of God is the sole cause of election. "The election of God is not, because he foresaw that we should do well, but the only cause of election is his mere mercy, and the cause of our doing well is his election."[2] In other words, a man is not chosen because of his good works, but he is able to perform truly good works only because he has been chosen. "Free will of its natural strength, without a special grace, can do nothing but abide in sin."[3]

To those who charged that this view of election portrayed God as unfair because he chose some and not others, Barnes retorted that God was not obliged to choose anyone. God, as sovereign, has every right to decide how he will deal with his creatures. All men are sinful and undeserving of God's goodness, so no one has reason to object to God's way of dealing with men. Furthermore, Barnes admonished his readers to believe that God "has treated you better than you deserve."[4]

Some of those who opposed the reformers cited passages of the Bible which teach that God wills the salvation of all men. In dealing with this argument, Barnes employed Luther's dichotomy between the *secret* and *revealed* wills of God:

> Consider that there are two manner of wills in God. One is called his . . . secret or inscrutable will, whereby all things are made and ordered. . . . Of this will no creature has knowledge. . . . It is sufficient for us to know . . . that there is an inscrutable will.
>
> The other will in God is called a declared and manifest will, which is declared and given to us in holy Scripture. . . . Men are bound to search and know this will, . . . and by this will is offered to every man those things that pertain to salvation. And by this will God will have no man damned, for he lets his word be preached indifferently to all men.[5]

In thus composing his argument, Barnes felt that he was giving all due honor to God. The tenor and content of his argument are like a page out of Luther's book, as even a cursory comparison will show.[6]

Like Luther, Barnes also believed that the doctrine of election had much more significance than simply that of a subject for academic disputation. Luther urged that this doctrine be preached for the "sweet comfort"[7] it held for troubled souls. Barnes agreed, stressing the assurance which one might enjoy from the knowledge of his election.

> First God comes, for the love of Christ Jesus, only of his mere mercy, and gives us freely the gift of faith whereby we do believe God, and his holy word, and stick fast unto the promises of God, and believe, that though heaven and earth and all that is in them should perish, . . . yet God shall be found true in his promises, for this faith's sake: we are the elect children of God.[8]

Although he did not compose a treatise specifically on the subject of election, William Tyndale frequently expressed his opinion about it in his theological and expository writings, as, for example, in his *Parable of the Wicked Mammon.* "In Adam we are all, as it were, wild crab trees, of which God chooses whom he will, and plucks them out of Adam and plants them in the garden of his mercy."[9]

In his prologue to the Epistle to the Romans, Tyndale exulted, "by . . . predestination our justifying and salvation are clean taken out of our hands and put in the hands of God alone."[10] In the same theocentric manner as Luther and Barnes, Tyndale then situated the ground of election completely in the will of God. Tyndale saw man as "full of that poison whence naturally all sins spring, and wherewith we cannot but sin."[11] Assuming this condition of utter spiritual inability, Tyndale concluded that there could never be any basis for election other than the decree of God. "The true believer . . . in Christ was predestinated and ordained unto eternal life, before the world began."[12]

William Tyndale asserted that this was the only view which excluded human boasting and extolled the glory of God. No man deserves God's predestinating love, and the fact that He bestows it without regard to human merit should humble the Christian and cause him to serve God with loving gratitude.[13]

Tyndale anticipated the arguments of the Semi-Pelagians by denying that free will enables man to choose God. To the contrary, he insisted, "God chooses them first, and not they God."[14] As Tyndale saw it, knowledge of one's election is the whole basis for spiritual security in the Christian life. It is the assurance of salvation through that divine mercy, which shall never be withdrawn from God's elect.[15]

Although he did not write extensively on the subject, Tyndale apparently felt that some knowledge of the doctrine of election was essential for an understanding of the over-all message of Scripture. This appears to be the case in his essay, *A Pathway into the Holy Scripture,* which he intended as an introduction for readers of his New Testament.[16]

The doctrine of predestination, or election, may not have been the central issue in the debate between English Catholics and Protestants in the early sixteenth century, but it was an important part of the controversy about salvation. The other aspects of the controversy are more readily understood if the disagreement on election is appreciated.

## JUSTIFICATION

In a sense, the reformers' doctrine of election was the summary of their view of God and man. If God is totally sovereign and man spiritually dead because of sin, the only hope for man must lie in the divine initiative. That is, God must save man — simply because man can neither save himself nor contribute anything toward his salvation. Salvation must be exclusively the work of God, and the reformers insisted that it was a work which he performed *sola gratia*.

In conformity with all Christian tradition, the reformers believed that God took the initiative in salvation when He entered history in the person of Jesus Christ. They all confessed that God literally became man "for us men, and for our salvation," as it was stated in the Nicene Creed. As Luther put it,

> I believe that Jesus Christ, true God, begotten of the Father from eternity, and also true man, born of the Virgin Mary, is my Lord; who has redeemed me, a lost and condemned creature, secured and delivered me from all sins, from death, and from the power of the devil, not with silver and gold, but with his holy and precious blood, . . . in order that I might be his, live under him in his kingdom, and serve him in everlasting righteousness, innocence and blessedness; even as he is risen from the dead, and lives and reigns to all eternity.[17]

Barnes and Tyndale did not state their understanding of the incarnation so eloquently, but they agreed with Luther and looked to the life, death, and resurrection of Christ as the cause of their salvation. Specifically, Luther and his followers focused upon the crucifixion of Christ as accomplishing a full atonement for the sins of the world.

The particular view which the reformers espoused was akin to that taught by Anselm of Canterbury (d. 1109) in his treatise *Cur Deus Homo*. Anselm maintained that God

115

could only forgive sin in a way that would be consistent with the essential holiness and righteousness of his character as reflected in his law. Man had violated the divine law, and God's honor and justice demanded satisfaction. Since man was contaminated by sin, his will consenting unto sin, there was no possibility that man could make the required satisfaction himself. For this reason, God became man in Christ to render satisfaction of the divine justice by assuming the penalty for sin, which was death. Christ's death atoned for the sins of others because He had no sin of His own. The innocent suffered for the guilty in order to relieve them of the eternal punishment due to sin. The reformers accepted the Anselmic view, but in their doctrine of the atonement they gave emphasis to the love of God and the necessity for personal faith, aspects which were ignored by Anselm.[18]

As Robert Barnes saw it, the atonement is the highest expression of the mercy and justice of God. Because of the atonement, undeserving sinners receive divine mercy, while Christ pays the penalty for sin, thus leaving God's justice unimpaired. Barnes counseled his readers:

> Though an angel would make you believe that all the world shall be damned, yet stick fast to his [God's] mercy and to his justice that justifies you, and believe that the sweet blood of his blessed Son cannot be shed in vain. Believe that it must justify sinners, as many as stick fast to it, though they be ever so blinded and ever so hardened, for it was shed only for them.[19]

One of the vital points in Tyndale's argument with Sir Thomas More was the reformer's accusation that the medieval Catholic teaching of salvation by ecclesiastical rites and human works denied the sufficiency of Christ's atonement.[20] Tyndale made his understanding of the atonement explicit in his *Exposition of the First Epistle of St. John* (1531). "Christ is our righteousness, our justifying, our redemption, our atonement, that has appeased God, and cleanses us from our sins, and all in his blood, so that his blood is the satisfaction only."[21]

It was because of the value they attached to the death of Christ that Barnes and Tyndale found the medieval cult of the saints intolerable. Tyndale defied anyone to show where the saints contributed one iota to the atonement,[22] and Barnes inveighed: "Either Christ does this thing [the atonement] alone, or else he is dead in vain, for he will have no helper."[23]

Once it is granted that the death of Christ made full atonement for sin, the question remains as to just how the benefits of his death may be appropriated to the life of the individual. On this matter, the unanimous and unchanging reply of Luther, Barnes, and Tyndale was to cite St. Paul: "The just shall live by faith" (Romans 1:17). Indeed, justification *sola fide* became a watchword of the Protestant Reformation.

Luther saw justification by faith as the bedrock of the Reformation. In the Smalkald Articles (1537) he wrote, "On this article rests all that we teach and practice. . . . Therefore, we must be quite certain and have no doubts about it. Otherwise all is lost, and the pope, the devil, and all our adversaries will gain the victory."[24]

Barnes was convinced that the doctrine of justification *sola fide* is the cord binding the entire Bible together. As he put it, "All Scripture is nothing else but a whole probation of this article."[25] Tyndale concluded, "It is impossible to understand either Peter or Paul, or anything in the scripture, for him that denies the justifying of faith in Christ's blood."[26] After a careful reading of the works of Barnes and Tyndale, the present writer must conclude that justification by faith was pivotal to their entire theology.

Because they regarded mankind as universally sinful and spiritually impotent, the reformers held that the faith by which a man is declared righteous, and therefore accepted in the sight of God, is itself a gift from God. As Luther explained it, "Faith . . . is a divine work in us which changes us and makes us to be born anew of God. . . . This faith God must give."[27] Tyndale phrased it: "True faith is the gift of God; and is given to sinners, after the law has passed upon them, and has brought their consciences to the brim of desperation and sorrows of hell."[28]

In medieval scholastic theology the Semi-Pelagian view of man had produced the teaching that man achieves right standing (justification) before God by his good works, even though those good works were made possible through "infused grace." The medieval view of justification put the emphasis on human merit. For the scholastics, "justification is not a judicial act of God; it is a gradual process of human recovery."[29] The process is a joint divine-human endeavor facilitated by meritorious human works.

The Reformation doctrines of divine sovereignty and human inability precluded any role for human works in the matter of justification. Luther saw justification as a once-for-all judicial act of God by which He declared all sinners righteous before the bar of divine justice. And the perfect righteousness of the sinless Christ was imputed to them. Those, then, who believe in Christ, by that same hand of faith lay hold of the righteousness of Christ — the only righteousness which qualifies a man to stand accepted in God's sight.[30] In a manner that defies comprehension, God declares as righteous men who are at the same time sinful.

This concept of justification reflects the essential theocentricity of Reformation theology. The reformers were convinced that theirs was the only understanding of justification which gave adequate glory to God. Luther summarized the scholastic view thus: "Human nature, corrupt and blinded by the blemish of original sin, is not able to imagine or conceive of any justification above and beyond works."[31]

The controversy between the scholastics and the reformers was partially due to confusion over the precise sense in which the Bible used the verb "to justify." Those whose only knowledge of the Bible came from the Latin Vulgate took the infinitive *justificare* to mean "to make righteous," and so concluded that justification is a process in which God and man co-operate. The reformers, however, made use of the Greek New Testament and discovered that *dikaioo* signifies "to count righteous." This was the translation which appeared in Tyndale's version.[32]

Believing that the honor and glory of God were at stake in the controversy of faith vs. works, the reformers attacked the partisans of Rome without mitigation. Barnes called St. Augustine into the fray as an ally against those who promoted works-righteousness. "Augustine condemns all your good works before faith and says that they are worth nothing, but vain and things out of the way."[33]

Tyndale was equally outspoken against the scholastic position. "How dark is the doctrine of those who [to the rebuke of Christ's blood] teach that works do justify before God and make satisfaction for sins!"[34]

The opponents of the Protestant theologians reacted to the righteousness-by-faith concept by charging that the teaching would encourage moral laxity by killing all incentive to do good works. This was a most serious charge, and it was fortified by evidence that some people had taken their

evangelical liberty from the law to mean that they were permitted the utmost moral license. This was an accusation
which the reformers could not ignore, and, to their credit,
they dealt with it forthrightly. They began their defense
with a careful definition of the "faith" which truly justifies
a sinner.

In his treatise *Onely fayth justifieth before God,* Robert
Barnes argued that, Biblically speaking, the only saving
faith is one which transforms a man. "Of a fleshly beast, it
makes me a spiritual man; of a damnable child, it makes me
a heavenly son; of a servant of the devil, it makes me a free
man of God."[35]

Barnes was intent upon showing that the reformers did
not regard faith as mere intellectual assent to the historic
verities of Christianity. Instead, he insisted that it was a
personal relationship of man to God, which produced intellectual and behavioral consequences of a salutary moral
character. Faith "must also make me believe that God . . . is
not only *a* father, but also *my* father: yes, and that through
the favor that Christ has purchased for me."[36]

Tyndale composed his major exposition of justification
*sola fide* in his *Parable of the Wicked Mammon,* though numerous references to this doctrine appear throughout his
published works. In fact, Tyndale wrote so often on this
theme that one interpreter has concluded rightly that it is
"in the light of this doctrine that his controversial teaching
must be viewed."[37] Defining what it means to have faith in
Christ, Tyndale wrote:

> The devil believes that Christ died, but not that he
> died for his sins. Neither does anyone who con-
> sents in the heart to continue in sin, believe that
> Christ died for him. For to believe that Christ died

for us is to see our horrible damnation, and . . . to
be sure that we are delivered therefrom through
Christ. In that we have power to hate our sins, and
to love God's commandments. All such repent and
have their hearts loosed out of captivity and bondage of sin, and are therefore justified through
faith in Christ.[38]

In so stating the Protestant position, Tyndale argued that
the grace of God produces twin responses when it is impressed upon the heart. These twin responses are faith and
repentance — inseparable characteristics of a true Christian. As Tyndale saw it, true faith in Christ repudiates sin
and sincerely desires to obey the law of God.[39] This was a
significant point in Tyndale's reply to More, for the latter
protested that justification *sola fide* must lead to moral
decay.

In the debate with More, Tyndale distinguished sharply
between a merely formal faith which nods assent to doctrinal propositions and a personal trust in Christ as one's own
Savior. Tyndale dissented from the medieval concept that
salvation is the reward for doctrinal conformity to the creed
adopted by the established Church. He argued that even
Satan might be doctrinally orthodox while completely lacking in personal saving faith.[40]

Tyndale also attacked Thomas More for advocating the
scholastic idea of "penance" rather than the Biblical teaching of "repentance." Penance was regarded as a sacrament
which absolved a confessing sinner of his guilt on the condition that he make satisfaction for his sins by means of prayer, fasting, pilgrimages, alms, etc. Once more, the emphasis
was upon human works to secure divine favor. Tyndale argued forcefully that the New Testament *metanoia* signifies

121

a change of heart and mind produced by divine grace whereby a man born in sin is brought to hate sin and love God. This, he insisted, is repentance — a work of God in the heart.[41]

In their exposition of justification by faith, the reformers also stressed the element of personal trust in Christ as opposed to unquestioning confidence in the institutional Church, as demanded by Rome. Barnes and Tyndale wrote complementary summaries which encompass this emphasis.

> If we truly confess Christ, then we must grant with our hearts that Christ is all our justice, all our redemption, all our wisdom, all our holiness, alone the peacemaker between God and man. . . . We have need of nothing toward our salvation, but of him only, and we desire no other salvation, nor any other satisfaction, nor any help of any other creature, either heavenly or earthly, but of him only.[42]

> Faith only, which is a sure and undoubted trust in Christ, and in the Father through him, certifies the conscience that the sin is forgiven, and the damnation and impossibility of the law taken away, . . . and with such persuasions mollifies the heart, and makes it love God again and his law.[43]

## THE CHRISTIAN LIFE

As was the case with predestination, the reformers' view of justification was not unprecedented in Church history. The writings of Augustine abound with affirmations of *sola fide*.[44] Nevertheless, the entrenched Semi-Pelagian religious establishment of the sixteenth century recoiled in horror when the reformers proposed their doctrine. The greatest expressed concern of the scholastics was that the Protestants, by disparaging good works, would lead people to ignore the laws of God and man. The apologists for medieval orthodoxy thought they detected a chaotic antinomianism in the Protestant view. They were especially alarmed at the suggestion that man could enjoy complete assurance of his salvation in this present life. The debates over election and justification were concomitants of this concern.

The reformers now had to show that their doctrine of salvation by faith in no way discouraged the performance of good works. Their position was that while truly good works are impossible without faith, genuine faith produces good works. As Luther put it in his *Theses Concerning Faith and Law* (1535), "good works must follow faith, yes, not only must, but follow voluntarily, just as a good tree not only must produce good fruits, but does so freely."[45] Good works then are the consequences rather than the cause of justification.

As the reformers saw it, the truly Christian life is one of good works. It is a *faith that works*. Good works are the index of faith and the evidence of salvation. Therefore they are a means of assurance for justified sinners. "Faith, the mother of all good works, justifies us, before we can bring forth any good work: as the husband marries his wife, before he can have any lawful children by her."[46] Or, as Barnes phrased it from the negative perspective, "those men who will do no good works because they are justified only by faith, are not the children of God, nor the children of justification."[47]

The reformers were confident that the correct understanding of justification would lead to a life of good works, for they held that the justified man was energized by the deepest of all possible motivations — love for the law of God. Therefore, the Christian life is characterized by a spontaneity of good works for the glory of God and the benefit of one's neighbor.[48] Tyndale directed his readers: "if you will be sure that your faith is perfect then examine yourself whether you love the law."[49] With great fervor, Tyndale urged believers to implement the moral and ethical principles of Christ's Sermon on the Mount as evidence of their "new and godly living fashioned after God's laws."[50] For Tyndale, "the transition [from spiritual death to spiritual life] comes by the gift of faith which immediately and almost by definition passes into love."[51]

Robert Barnes, in good Lutheran fashion, emphasized that since the Christian is not required to work for his salvation, he will devote his energies to serving the needs of his fellow man. A just man will do good works "to serve his brother, for he has no need of them concerning his justification."[52] At this point Barnes took the Epistle of James to teach that a Christian's good works are the identification of his justification before men,[53] the Augustinian conclusion with which Tyndale concurred.[54] Tyndale agreed that justification by faith produces a horizontal impact, that is, it leads man to love and serve his neighbor.[55]

Although the reformers cited love for God and His law as the primary motivation for good works, they did not conclude that truly good works receive no reward. Barnes and Tyndale asserted with all the energy they could muster that salvation is a gift from God, and, in no sense, a reward for human effort. Good works performed in faith and love, however, will receive suitable recompense, "though remission of sins and justification are not the reward referred to."[56] Oddly, Barnes did not elaborate on the nature of such rewards. Tyndale was more precise. He maintained that good works aid in the pursuit of real holiness and strengthen faith and the assurance of one's election.[57]

Another necessary consequence of their doctrine of justification was the reformers' rejection of the medieval dichotomy between the religious life and the secular life. Where the medieval Church exalted monasticism as the highest expression of piety, the reformers assailed it as a cloak for the most terrible hypocrisies.

Like Luther, the early English reformers taught that it is God who places men in various vocations, and the labor of one is not more spiritual than that of another. Tyndale said that God did not value an apostle more highly than a shoemaker or a kitchen-page. "All works are good which are done within the law of God, in faith, and with thanksgiving to God."[58] Where the Romanists regarded the clergy as comprising a professional ministry, Tyndale spoke of the "ministry" of one who washes dishes. "If you compare deed to deed, there is a difference between washing dishes and preaching the word of God; but as touching to please God, none at all."[59]

Faith and love may be demonstrated even by mundane tasks which render a common service to one's neighbor.

As indicated, both Barnes and Tyndale attacked the clergy for their failure to aid the suffering poor. This was not merely a feature of the reformers' anticlericalism but also an aspect of their view of the Christian life, for a social dimension of their ethics is clearly discernible in the records. Martin Luther asked that each city establish machinery for the relief of its poor through the maintenance of a "common chest."[60] Tyndale explicitly said, "God has given one man riches, to help another in need."[61] He further concluded that a man who refuses to aid his needy neighbor is a thief. The man truly justified by faith will not ignore another man's plight. Tyndale expressed these convictions in his *Parable of the Wicked Mammon,* a treatise mainly dealing with justification by faith.[62]

Robert Barnes, perhaps more than any English reformer of his generation, emphasized the social responsibilities of the Christian life of good works. He urged the advocates of image-veneration to honor God through serving man.

> Do well unto man who is made in the image of God. Give him honour and reverence; give him meat when he is hungry; give him drink when he is thirsty; clothe him when he is naked; serve him when he is sick; give him lodging when he is a stranger; and when he is in prison, minister to his needs.[63]

Barnes also argued that considerations of charity must have priority over legal rights in the truly Christian life. He urged creditors not to seek the ultimate penalties of the law against impoverished debtors. As Barnes saw it, the true Christian will forgive the debts of those too poor to pay. His defense of the poor sometimes took the form of attacks against the influential wealthy, even at considerable risk to himself.[64] Robert Barnes, however, did not compose any plan for the systematic relief of the poor as advocated by Luther.

The evidence is abundant that the early English reformers in no way intended to discourage the performance of good works. On the contrary, they insisted that truly good works are the necessary consequences of justification by faith. Tyndale summarized their thinking. "Where right faith is, it brings forth good works: if there follow no good works, it is (no doubt) but a dream and an opinion, or feigned faith."[65]

Although the reformers taught that sinners were declared perfectly righteous in their standing before God by faith in Christ, they recognized that the Christian's life on earth is not sinless. Instead, they depicted the Christian life as a spiritual struggle between the new nature in Christ and the old sinful nature inherited from Adam. Because the Christian possesses both natures, he is caught in the tension between them.

In their understanding of this aspect of the Christian life, the early English reformers again revealed their indebtedness to Martin Luther. Their German mentor described the Christian experience in terms of a paradox — the believer is *simul iustus et peccator* — "those who have been justified in Christ are not sinners and are sinners nevertheless."[66] That is, because they have received the perfect righteousness of Christ by faith, true Christians are accounted as sinless by a judicial act of God. In actual experience, however, the believer is still "by nature sinful and unclean" and subject to temptations which appeal to his sinful flesh (nature), which remains within him. The struggle continues until death ends all temptation and the flesh is discarded. One of the hallmarks of the Christian life, according to Luther, is the Christian's fight against the appetites of his old Adam.[67]

William Tyndale and Robert Barnes did not coin any phrases comparable to *simul iustus et peccator,* but their writings show that they held that concept. Tyndale put it succinctly. "Every man is two men, flesh and spirit; which so fight perpetually one against another, that a man must go either back or forward, and cannot stand long in one state."[68] When the "flesh" (Luther's *peccator*) prevails, the believer sins. His sin, however, will be followed by sincere repentance, because the new nature of "spirit" (Luther's *iustus*) does not consent to sin.[69] Sins of weakness committed by one who has been justified through faith in Christ are "venial," not deadly sins. That is, they do not lead to damnation.[70]

## THE ROLE OF THE LAW IN THE CHRISTIAN LIFE

Until recently, interpreters of the early English Reformation have been satisfied to regard Robert Barnes and William Tyndale as primarily English disciples of Martin Luther. Barnes has traditionally been portrayed as a thoroughgoing Lutheran theologian, while it has been customary to regard Tyndale as Lutheran on all but a few points of doctrine, most notably, the sacraments.[71] The latest interpretive scholarship, however, is inclined to believe that some significant deviations from Luther may be observed in the works of Tyndale especially, and, to a lesser extent, in those of Barnes. Since the revisionists build their case mainly on the role of the divine law in the Christian life as Tyndale and Barnes understood it, it is fitting to close this study of their concept of salvation with an examination of this matter.

Among the advocates of the revisionist approach are William A. Clebsch, L. J. Trinterud, and John K. Yost.[72] The work of Clebsch has probably had the broadest impact to date. In order that we may have a standard of judgment with which to evaluate the newer interpretation, it would be well first of all to survey Luther's position on the role of the law in the Christian life.

From the discussion on justification by faith it will be apparent that Luther held that the divine law has nothing to contribute to salvation. The law rather exposes man's sinfulness and inability to fulfill the divine requirements. It issues demands but does not impart power for compliance. A man is declared righteous solely by faith in Christ. Does the divine law, then, have no relevance for the Christian? On the contrary, it has great relevance, for, in addition to the theological function of the law as bringing condemnation for sin, there is the civil function of the law to restrain evil. The Christian has been freed by Christ from the condemnation of the law but still needs the law's civil restraint.

The believer's need for the civil use of the law exists because he is *simul iustus et peccator* — at one and the same time righteous and sinful. His new righteous nature requires no restraint of the law, but his old sinful nature still needs the law to expose and restrain his sinfulness. The law serves to encourage the Christian to renew his repentance continually. Because all men are sinful by nature, civil society could not endure without the law, and the Christian is a participant in civil society.[73] Furthermore, the New Testament contains many commandments which serve to encourage the Christian to perform good works.[74]

Probably the most important expression of Luther's belief in the relevance of the law for the Christian is reflected in the fact that a major portion of his two catechisms expound the Ten Commandments.

Luther held that the Ten Commandments really contain the same moral principles as the "natural law," that is, the law written in the human heart as part of the image of God. Therefore, this moral law is universally applicable. "Why does one . . . keep and teach the Ten Commandments? . . . Because the natural laws were never so orderly and well written as by Moses."[75]

Rather than say unequivocally that the divine law is the essential code of Christian behavior, Martin Luther taught that, insofar as the Christian man is righteous, he needs no law. His love for God will prompt him to do God's will with spontaneity.[76] Later Lutheranism, and, to an even greater extent, Calvinism, did not hesitate to speak of the law as the Christian moral code.

Now, to return to the early English reformers, we are confronted with the opinion that Barnes and Tyndale parted company with Luther on the issue of the law. Clebsch speaks of Barnes' "enrolling in 1531 as a theological disciple of Luther, and of his liberation by 1534 from that master,"[77] while "Tyndale introduced into his theology a second theological use of law, and thereby renounced his discipleship to Luther."[78]

Professor Clebsch feels that their un-Lutheran concept of the law was especially apparent in Barnes' and Tyndale's attitude toward the Epistle of James. As shown previously,[79] both of these reformers accepted James as canonical Scripture, explaining James' teaching on justification by works to apply to the demonstration of faith before men. Clebsch concludes that, in the case of Tyndale, he assumed a moralistic and legalistic interpretation of Christianity "as the divine capacitation of man to fulfill the ethical injunctions of the Old and New Testaments."[80] Moreover, Clebsch insists that Tyndale finally made the concept of the covenant, as a contract binding God and man in mutual obligation, the organizing principle of his theology. This, according to Clebsch, represents a definite break with Luther.[81] For Tyndale, "the object of religion was morality. Here Tyndale was actually far closer to the Catholic humanists of England, such as Colet or Fisher or Gardiner or even More, than he was to Luther."[82]

L. J. Trinterud sees Tyndale's view that justification brings love for the law of God and ability to keep the law as incompatible with Luther's teaching that love for God and man would allow the Christian to transcend the law. Trinterud holds that Tyndale was a covenant theologian whose position reflects greater affinity with the doctrines of the Reformed (Calvinists), than with Luther.[83]

John K. Yost, like Clebsch, concludes that Tyndale was actually a humanist who "desired most of all to rediscover . . . the New Testament conception of the law of God and the ethical wisdom of earliest Christianity."[84] Yost feels that this emphasis is especially apparent in Tyndale's position on James, and in his exposition of the Sermon on the Mount.

The present writer's study of Barnes and Tyndale for the most part has not confirmed the revisionist position. Barnes and Tyndale may not have echoed some of Luther's negative remarks about the canonicity of James, but this hardly means that they were necessarily renouncing Luther. Justification *sola fide* before God was the cornerstone of the Reformation, both German and English. Nowhere in the writings of Barnes and Tyndale is there evidence to suggest that either ever abandoned this doctrine.

It is true that Tyndale saw love for the law of God as an essential distinguishing characteristic of a true Christian. It is also true that he believed that God gave his elect motivation and power to keep the divine law. But one must ask just how this contradicts Luther's position? Luther simply said that the Christian's love for God demonstrated itself by good works which accord with divine law.[85]

Even in the matter of the covenant as binding God and man in mutual obligation, there is no irreconcilable disagreement between Luther and Tyndale if one keeps in mind that both reformers presupposed that only those with faith in Christ could enjoy a covenant relationship with God. Tyndale expounded on his idea of the covenant in his *Exposition of the First Epistle of St. John* (1531), a work that

repeatedly affirms justification by faith.[86] One need only
compare Luther and Tyndale on the covenant concept to see
their compatibility. First Tyndale:

> God . . . has made appointment between him and
> us, in Christ's blood; and has bound himself to give
> us whatsoever we ask in his name, testifying
> thereto . . . that he will be a father unto us, and
> save us both in this life and in the life to come, and
> take us from under the damnation of the law, and
> set us under grace and mercy, . . . and though at a
> time we mar all through our infirmity, yet, if we
> turn again, that shall be forgiven us mercifully . . .
> which testament [covenant] is confirmed with
> signs and wonders through the Holy Spirit.[87]

Luther expressed himself on essentially the same theme
in a treatise of 1521:

> God has made a covenant with those who are in
> Christ, so that there is no condemnation if they
> fight against themselves and their sin.[88]

Both Luther and Tyndale subscribed unyieldingly to justification before God *sola fide*. Their similar ideas on the
covenant in no way detracted from the importance they attached to justification. Both saw participants in the covenant relationship as justified believers whose manner of life
is characterized by a struggle against temptation and their
old sinful nature.

In the light of this evidence, one wonders about the opinion of Clebsch when he says that Tyndale's later expositions
portray God "as a reliable negotiator of agreements who
bound himself to the terms of a contract."[89] Tyndale's doctrine of divine sovereignty simply does not allow for an interpretation which depicts God as negotiating with His

creatures. The covenant concept of Luther and Tyndale features the sovereign God making promises to men who abide by His Word, but the covenant originates exclusively with God, who then hands it down to man. Tyndale's exact words were, "God . . . has made an appointment . . . ," while Luther said, "God has made a covenant . . . " The idea of God as "negotiator" is foreign to the thought of both reformers. God conceived the covenant, and He prescribed its terms.

One is also puzzled by Clebsch's suggestion that Tyndale was actually closer in belief to Thomas More than to Martin Luther. It is quite evident that More did not think so. One need only scan the *Confutation of Tyndale's Answer* to see that More regarded his opponent as a purveyor of Lutheran heresy.[90] More saw the practice of good morality as the means to salvation, but Tyndale insisted that good morality was impossible until one was first justified by faith. As Tyndale's leading biographer has incisively observed:

> The conflict between the two men might almost be summed up in More's hairshirt. If Tyndale had known of this, he would have regarded it as a mere treatment of symptoms, a timid negative measure, which at best could do no more than distract a man from evil thoughts, but was powerless to liberate within him desires of active goodness.[91]

Equally unconvincing as the arguments of Clebsch, are those of Yost. It is futile to brand Tyndale as an Erasmian humanist, as Yost has done. The Erasmians held to the Semi-Pelagian view of human nature, a view castigated by Tyndale, especially in his debate with More. Although Tyndale was earnestly concerned to promote good morality through obedience to divine law, he never wavered from his teaching that justification by faith is the prerequisite. Man

133

cannot truly obey the law until he comes to love it, and only faith in Christ enables him to do so.

Trinterud is more cautious in describing Tyndale's movement away from Luther. He correctly shows that Tyndale gave greater prominence and emphasis to the role of the law in the Christian life than Luther did. Perhaps there is some reason to conclude, as Trinterud has done, that on this one point, Tyndale was closer to the later Calvinists than to Luther.

In an earlier article Trinterud cited Tyndale as one of the forefathers of English Puritanism.[92] The "covenant" idea is certainly present in Tyndale's writings, and it is likely that he helped to prepare the way for the mature covenant theology of the seventeenth century Puritans. Tyndale did hold that the divine covenant promises were made to those who obeyed the conditions laid down by God, but, as shown in our answer to Clebsch, the germ of this concept was also present in Luther's thinking, though he did not develop it as fully as Tyndale. Both Luther and Tyndale would insist that the only ones who would fulfill the covenant requirements were those who had already been justified by faith. Covenant-keeping in Reformation theology was viewed as being among the consequences rather than part of the cause of salvation. Faith alone justifies before God, and it must precede all truly good works.

There is one piece of evidence which the revisionists seem to have overlooked in their efforts to detach Tyndale from Luther. As we have seen earlier,[93] Tyndale early adopted Luther's Law-Gospel distinction as an exegetical principle for correct interpretation of the Bible. The revisionists claim that the mature Tyndale replaced this Lutheran concept with the covenant scheme. Once more, the present writer must dissent.

We have already shown that "covenant" talk is found in Luther. Furthermore, in the last year of his life, Tyndale sent a letter to John Frith which clearly shows that he still advocated the Law-Gospel concept. The letter bears quoting at length:

> Expound the law truly, and open the veil of Moses to condemn all flesh; and prove all men sinners, and all deeds under the law, before mercy has taken away the condemnation thereof, to be sin and damnable; and then, as a faithful minister, set abroad the mercy of our Lord Jesus, and let wounded consciences drink of the water of him. And then shall your preaching be with power, and not as the doctrine of the hypocrites; and the Spirit of God shall work with you, and all consciences shall bear record that it is so. And all doctrine that casts a mist on those two and hides them (I mean the law of God and mercy of Christ) that resist with all your power.[94]

Every theological element espoused in the above letter agrees with Luther's position. There are differences between Luther and Tyndale, and, to a lesser extent, between Luther and Barnes. Those differences, however, are relatively slight in the areas cited by the revisionists. Like Tyndale, Robert Barnes went beyond Luther by explicitly identifying the law in Scripture as a code of Christian conduct.[95] This should not be construed as a rejection of Luther, however. The didactic use of the law advocated by Barnes and Tyndale was really a logical extension of Luther's position. They expounded and applied the divine law in much the same way that Luther did in his catechisms.

## CHAPTER 6

# THE QUESTION OF THE CHURCH

## THE NATURE OF THE CHURCH

Inseparably connected with the Reformation controversy over salvation was the debate regarding the nature and function of the Church. By the sixteenth century, the Catholic Church had become a vast international organization administered by bishops under the direction of the pope. The bishops were viewed as successors to the New Testament apostles,and the pope as the successor to St. Peter, the traditional first Bishop of Rome, and, therefore, the visible head of the Church on earth. But the matter of authority had not been entirely settled. The question of papal vs. conciliar primacy agitated the late medieval Church at the same time that it was engaged in the confrontation with Protestantism.[1]

Although a distinction between the Church as a visible organization and the Church as a spiritual body of Christians did exist in medieval theology, it was not the same distinction as that made by the reformers. In medieval thought the visible Church was regarded mainly as the earthly body of people associated together in the Catholic fold and customarily called the Church militant. The invisible Church was composed of those in purgatory — the Church expectant; and those in heaven — the Church triumphant. Medieval Catholic thought apparently viewed the extant ecclesiastical organization on earth, *per se,* as the Church.[2]

Led by Luther, the reformers proposed a doctrine of the Church which differed sharply from the medieval teaching. In a treatise entitled *Concerning the Ministry* (1532), Luther defined the Church as the community of believers bound together by the Word of God. "Since the church owes its birth to the Word, is nourished, aided and strengthened by it, it is obvious that it cannot be without the Word. If it is without the Word it ceases to be a church."[3]

Luther held that the true Church is in a line of apostolic succession — not necessarily lineal, but doctrinal. That is, he believed that real apostolic succession was not a historical organizational connection with the primitive Church, but adherence to apostolic teaching from the Word. As Luther summarized it,

> In this Christian Church, wherever it exists, is to be found the forgiveness of sins, *i.e.,* a kingdom of grace and true pardon. For in it are found the gospel, baptism, and the sacrament of the altar, in which the forgiveness of sins is offered, obtained, and received. Moreover, Christ and his Spirit and God are there. Outside this Christian Church there is no salvation or forgiveness of sins, but everlasting death and damnation.[4]

It is clear from this and other writings that Luther saw two primary visible marks, or characteristics, of the Church. The first was the proclamation of God's Word through preaching, and the second was the proclamation of that same Word through the two sacraments. Subsidiary to these, the chief marks of the Church, Luther cited further distinguishing, though uncertain, features such as prayer, suffering persecution, the power of the "keys," and obedience to the Word on the part of Christian people.[5]

According to Luther, the Church cannot be confined to any one outward ecclesiastical organization, as, for example, the papacy. The true Church is universal, and its catholicity consists in its ministry of the Word and sacraments regardless of the context in which that ministry is performed.[6]

As Luther saw it, a lack of saving faith makes it impossible for one to comprehend the presence and nature of the Church. As a result of spiritual blindness most men regard the Church as a visible ecclesiastical hierarchy dominated by the pope and his clergy.[7] The spiritually blind bow before the Roman hierarchy in accord with the dictum of Thomas Aquinas that salvation requires obedience to the Roman pontiff.[8] According to Luther, the Church is the body of the elect, the invisible assembly of all believers in Christ, present wherever the Word and sacraments are administered according to the command of Christ.

Because faith is invisible, Luther held that no ecclesiastical organization is competent to determine whether or not a person has faith. This is not to say, however, that all ecclesiastical organization should be abandoned. Quite to the contrary, Luther was unsparing in his denunciation of radical sects which called for an extreme individualism that would forsake the visible Church.[9]

Luther taught that believers should gather together around the Word and sacraments. When they do so, they form a visible body confessing its faith — a church. The precise form of organization which such a body may assume is optional. Luther did not believe that any one form of church government was a divine requirement, a belief which widened the chasm separating him from Rome. To the present, world Lutheranism functions under a number of forms of church polity.

Luther's rather elastic view of polity was inseparably connected with his understanding of the priesthood. He ada-
mantly rejected the medieval tradition that ordination im-

LEFT: Philip Melanchthon   RIGHT: Dr. Luther

pressed an indelible grace upon a clergyman, elevating him from the "secular" to the "sacred" life. Instead, he argued, "all Christians are priests in equal degree."[10] By Biblical exegesis he asserted the New Testament teaching — all Christians have direct access to Christ. Therefore, they are all priests. The powers which the medieval Church claimed as a clerical monoply Luther saw as committed by God to the entire Church. Luther asserted that the preaching of the Word and the ministry of the sacraments have been entrusted to the Church as a body, and any believer authorized by the body may perform these services. Those designated by the body to perform them on a regular basis are "ministers," or servants, not priests.[11]

Since he saw no distinction between clergy and laity, except a difference in the function of their offices, Luther utterly rejected the Roman Catholic claim that spiritual authority resides with the professional priesthood through the power of the "keys." It is recorded in the Gospel according to St. Matthew (16:18) that Jesus said, "I will give you the keys of the kingdom of heaven; what you bind on earth shall be bound in heaven, and what you loose on earth shall be loosed in heaven." Christ addressed these words to the Apostle Peter in the presence of His other disciples, and from this text there arose the Roman doctrine of Petrine supremacy.

Rome taught that the "binding and loosing," pertaining to the forgiveness or retention of sins, belong exclusively to Peter, as the first pope, and to his pontifical successors — that they possess this supreme spiritual authority, which they exercise through the ordained priesthood. For hundreds of years loyal children of Rome confessed their sins to their priests in the quest for absolution through the sacrament of penance.

In 1520 Luther assailed the clerical claim to the exclusive possession of the "keys." In his treatise, *The Babylonian Captivity of the Church,* Luther argued from the Scriptures (Matthew 16) that the power of the keys was actually conveyed to the entire Church. Therefore the existence of the practice of sacerdotal absolution is a gross deprivation of Christian liberty. It is one of the devices by which Rome keeps men in spiritual bondage. Luther would have Christians confess to one another. "The sinner may make his sins known to whomever he will and seek pardon and comfort, that is, the word of Christ, by the mouth of his neighbor."[12] All Christians have the Word of God, so they may proclaim forgiveness of sins through the Gospel.[13]

The Church, then, as defined by Martin Luther, is the body of the elect, joined together in the ministry of the Word and sacraments. It is a body in which all believers are priests holding the power of the keys.

With Luther's view in the background, it is appropriate to compare the early English reformers' understanding of the nature of the Church.

## ROBERT BARNES ON THE CHURCH

One need not read far into the writings of Robert Barnes to discover that ecclesiology, or the doctrine of the Church, was a matter of foremost concern in his thinking. On the nature of the Church he defined his beliefs fully and clearly in a treatise entitled *What the Church is: and who bee thereof: and whereby men may know her.*[14]

In this treatise Barnes announced that his purpose in defining the Church was to expose the corruption and hypocrisy of the ecclesiastical institution. In places, Barnes' doctrine of the Church is actually more pointedly anti-Roman than that of Luther.

Like Martin Luther, Robert Barnes held that the true Church is invisible, and that, visibly speaking, it has certain marks which identify its presence in the world. The foundation of the Church is the Word of God; without it no religious body may rightly claim to be part of Christ's Church. "Where the Word of God is preached truly, it is a good and perfect token that there are some men of Christ's Church."[15] It is significant that Barnes said "*some* men of Christ's Church" are present where the Word is preached. This is a reflection of his belief that the true Church is ultimately invisible — known only to God.

Barnes also believed that even in assemblies where the Word is truly preached there will be people who will not receive it in faith. These people might associate themselves with a visible group of believers, but, since they do not receive the Word in faith, they are not members of that invisible Church known only to God. The Church known by God "is a spiritual thing, and not an exterior thing, but invisible from carnal eyes . . . as faith is."[16]

Because no man or body of men can infallibly perceive the presence or absence of faith, the Church on earth will include true believers and hypocrites. In the invisible Church, however, only the believers hold membership. This is the Bride of Christ. "Here we have the very true Church of Christ, that is so pure and clean without spot."[17] The blood of Christ has cleansed her, and the merits of Christ establish her righteousness. Indispensable for membership in the Church is personal faith in Christ as the Savior from sin. "They that believe that Christ washed from them their sins, and stick fast to his merits, . . . they are the Church of God."[18]

In connection with his attacks on William Tyndale, Sir Thomas More also rebuked Robert Barnes. This led Barnes to compose a treatise "wherein he answereth to Maister More."[19] In this brief essay Barnes summarized the marks of the true Church as he saw them. These marks include the preaching of the pure Word of God, the dispensing of the sacraments, the patient suffering of Christian people for the sake of God's truth, and the application of Biblical doctrine in the form of godly living.[20] The similarity between Barnes and Luther at this point is obvious.

In citing the suffering of believers as a mark of the Church, Barnes was again expressing his opposition to clericalism. He categorically denied that those bishops who opposed him had any place in the true Church. His point was that the true Church suffers oppression, while his episcopal adversaries regularly engaged in persecuting true Christian teachers as "heretics."[21]

Robert Barnes also believed that the true Church is catholic, or universal, but he did not equate universality with uniformity of structure or practice. In opposition to the claims of Rome he wrote: "The Holy Spirit is free, and inspires where he will. He will neither be bound to pope nor cardinal; archbishop nor bishop; abbot nor prior."[22] Therefore, no one pattern of church government is essential to its ministry of the Word and sacraments. Barnes was willing to accept the episcopal administration of the visible Church, provided that the Word was preached and the sacraments rightly dispensed, and abuses corrected. He was not optimistic, however, that this was going to occur. His disgust with the religious establishment was probably the reason he wrote very little on the matter of church government.[23]

Although Barnes' opposition to clericalism was provoked by the ecclesiastical abuses so prevalent in his day, the theoretical basis of his criticism of the professional clergy was derived from his doctrine of the priesthood. Employing

the arguments of Luther, Barnes taught that all believers
are priests before God and the clergy merely servants appointed by their congregations to the ministry of the Word
and sacraments.[24] He was caustic and explicit in rejecting
the medieval clergy-laity distinction.

> Whether they be Jew or Greek, king or subject,
> carter or cardinal, butcher or bishop, water boy or
> street sweeper, free or bond, friar or fiddler, monk
> or miller; if they believe in Christ's Word and stick
> fast to his blessed promises, and trust only in the
> merits of his blessed blood, they are the holy
> Church of God, yes and the very true Church of
> God.[25]

Because he saw the Church as a universal priesthood of
believers, Barnes continually assailed the clergy for jealous-
ly guarding their traditional professional privileges. When
the clerics argued that accessibility to the Scriptures in the
vernacular would make people heretics, Barnes' rejoinder
was that they simply defined heresy as speaking against
their unscriptural laws and practices.[26]

Perhaps more than anywhere else in his writings, Robert
Barnes' adherence to the concept of the priesthood of all believers was made patently clear in his essay, *What the keys
of the Church bee, and to whom they were geuen.*[27] Reading
this treatise, the clerics of the established Church could not
fail to conclude that Barnes was a subversive threat to the
entire ecclesiastical order. His essay was as much an attack
upon his opponents as an exposition of the doctrine.

Robert Barnes took the relevant Scripture passage in
Matthew 16 to teach that Christ intended that all Chris-
tians should possess the "keys of the kingdom," and that
Peter merely received them as the representative of the

whole Church. The keys "are the common treasure of the Church and belong no more to one man than to another."[28] Barnes held that the Word of God is the key which brings forgiveness of sins, and it was committed to the entire Church to be proclaimed by all Christians as servants of God. Citing St. Augustine and St. John Chrysostom in support, Barnes declared: "This holy Word is the very true key of heaven, for by it heaven is opened and shut."[29]

In expounding on the question of the keys, Barnes appealed to apostolic precedent as deciding the manner in which the power of the keys may be legitimately employed. He said that the Apostles preached the Word of God, which loosed men from their sins when received in faith, and bound them when rejected in unbelief. This, insisted Barnes, is the only way in which the keys may be employed.[30]

Barnes was especially repelled by the Catholic teaching that the power of the keys gave the clergy the prerogative of admitting or excluding souls from heaven by ecclesiastical action such as excommunication. Although the Church may commit the ministry of preaching to learned men, these men "are but ministers of the common treasure, and not lords over it."[31] He indicted the clerics of his day for usurping authority not implicit in the doctrine of the keys, castigating their motives as well as their practices. "All that you do is clearly done for money and no other cause,"[32] he charged, alluding to the sale of relics and other commercial features of popular religion.

In rejecting the Catholic teaching that clerical ordination impresses an indelible character upon a priest, Barnes called for the removal of clerics who do not discharge their ministry well. Since it was the Church that installed them as ministers, the Church may depose them as well.

There was one feature of his ecclesiology in which Robert Barnes differed slightly from Martin Luther, and it was mainly a matter of emphasis. Luther always cited the Word and sacraments as marks of the true Church; on occasion he listed a few secondary distinguishing features, among them, the obedience of Christians to God's Word.[33] But the latter was not a point on which Luther was at all emphatic. In fact, he hesitated to regard the good works of believers as a sign of the Church. Considering the nature of man, he felt that good works were not sufficiently constant and abundant to regard them as a mark of the Church without qualification.[34]

On the matter of listing the good works of Christians as a sign of the true Church, Robert Barnes had no hesitation. Perhaps this is a reflection of his didactic use of the law in the Christian life, which, as indicated,[35] was another question on which he did not remain strictly within the bounds of Luther's teaching.

Before concluding this inquiry into Robert Barnes' concept of the nature of the Church, it is fitting to appraise his role as a church historian. Barnes earned distinction as the first Protestant historian of the papacy with his *Vitae Romanorum Pontificum* of 1535.[36]

Barnes' *Lives of the Roman Popes*, unfortunately, has little value. It covers the period from the Apostles to Alexander III (d.1181), listing 175 pontiffs. Some of those included have since been removed from the official list of popes by the Roman Catholic Church. The only popes on the list to receive significant coverage are those who were noteworthy for their relations with England. It is interesting to see that Clebsch puts this piece of Barnes' writing under the sub-heading "Scissors and Paste," and then concludes, "the entire work . . . was merely a catena of standard medieval and renaissance sources, to which Barnes brought the originality only of selection."[37]

The tenor of the *Vitae Romanorum Pontificum* shows clearly that it is history written for polemical purposes. In it Barnes indicted the medieval Church for allowing the accretion of non-scriptural liturgical practices.

> The rites of the mass were multiplied in the course of time. Celestine added the introit, Gregory the *Kyrie eleison*. Telesphorus the *Gloria in excelsis Deo*, Galasius the collects, Jerome the Epistle and Gospel. The *Alleluia* was taken from the church of Jerusalem. The Nicene Council added the creed, Pelagius the commemoration of the dead, Leo III incense, Innocent the kiss of peace, Sergius the *Agnus Dei*. What the other pontiffs added will be told for each in his own place.[38]

The translator of the above passage sees Barnes as unwittingly leading the way for a later Zwinglian-style anti-ceremonialism, which reached maturity in Puritanism.[39] This conclusion appears justified, for Barnes tended to disparage any ritual or ceremony which lacked specific Biblical precedent. In this he differed sharply from Luther, who generally held that ceremonies not contradicted by Scripture were permissible.[40]

## WILLIAM TYNDALE ON THE CHURCH

In discoursing upon the doctrine of the Church, William Tyndale gave priority to the exegesis of the pivotal passage in Matthew 16. Because of the importance which he attached to the interpretation of this text, it is appropriate to quote it in full. There it is recorded that Jesus said: "You are Peter, and upon this rock I will build my church; and the gates of hell shall not prevail against it."

Since in Greek *petros* means a rock, traditional Catholic interpretation cited this text as the major basis for the claim that Peter was the first pope, upon whom the Church was founded. Furthermore, the Roman apologists argued that all subsequent popes were in a line of apostolic succession from Peter, and, therefore, invested with the same primacy of authority which he enjoyed.

By comparing Scripture with Scripture, Tyndale understood the "rock" of Matthew 16:18 in a three-fold sense: "Now says all the scripture, that the rock is Christ, the faith, and God's word."[41] The Church, then, is the congregation of true believers built by faith upon the Word of God. To say without qualification that Peter is the rock is to speak the language of Antichrist.[42]

In denying that Peter was the rock, Tyndale intended no slight to the Apostle. On the contrary, he explained that Peter's confession of faith in Christ was representative of the faith of the true Church. "This faith is the rock, whereon Christ's Church is built."[43] Membership in this true Church is limited to those who trust Christ by faith.

Much of what Tyndale said about ecclesiology appeared in his debate with Thomas More. There Tyndale defined the Church as embracing all believing clergy and laity throughout the world, "in whose hearts God has written his law with his Holy Spirit, and given them a feeling faith in the mercy that is in Christ Jesus our Lord."[44] In this way, Tyndale rejected the scholastic idea that the term "Church" had special reference to the clergy. He translated the Greek *ecclesia* as "congregation" in order to counteract the scholastic opinion.

As did Luther and Barnes, Tyndale distinguished between the visible and invisible Church. He held that the call of the Gospel attracts many outward adherents who really do not embrace Christ by faith. Such people may outwardly give assent to the creedal position of Christianity intellectually but be lacking that faith which makes one a real Christian. Specifically, Tyndale charged that the millions of professing Christians who seek salvation through their works are in this category. They belong only to the "fleshly" earthly Church, and not to the true "spiritual" invisible Church.[45] Because the pope teaches men to trust in the efficacy of works and ceremonies, he and his disciples have no part in the true Church.[46] The partisans of Rome, according to Tyndale, are "popish hypocrites . . . who need . . . a John the Baptist to convert them."[47]

Even excluding the papists, however, Tyndale held that the Church on earth is fettered by the sin of its members. Because of justification by faith, the true Church is judicially righteous and pure before God. In actual experience, however, Christians still sin. Therefore, the Church as a body is in the same condition as the individual believer — *simul iustus et peccator,* as Luther phrased it.[48]

Apparently, Tyndale did not resort to a succinct dictum such as Luther's "Word and sacrament" to epitomize the marks of the true Church. With Luther and Barnes, he surely regarded the preaching of the Word and the ministry of the sacraments as essential to the Church, and, also like his two co-laborers in reform, he listed a number of other distinguishing features of the true Church.

Tyndale argued against More that the Church is the child of the Word of God, and not the Word the child of the Church. Tyndale's position was that faith makes one a Christian, and Christians compose the Church, *ergo* faith came through the Word before the Church was composed. The order is Word-faith-Church. Tyndale knew full well that the Church was functioning before the inscripturation of the Word was completed, but he held that the Word was orally proclaimed at that time and so still preceded the Church.[49]

As Tyndale saw it, the true Church would also be identified by the sufferings it endured at the hands of false Christians. With a mixture of lament and irony he wrote: "The fleshly shall persecute the spiritual, as Cain did Abel, . . . and the great multitude shall persecute the small little flock, and Antichrist will be ever the best Christian man."[50] In other words, the elect would be a tiny minority surrounded by a host of false "Christians," who oppress them for their adherence to the truth. The numerical inferiority of real believers Tyndale saw as another sign of the true Church.[51]

In the midst of his dispute with More, Tyndale summarized his view of the true Church in its standing before God.

> I believe that every soul that repents, believes, and loves the law, is through faith a member of Christ's Church, and pure, without spot or wrinkle, as Paul affirms (Ephesians V): and it is an article of my belief, that Christ's elect Church is holy and pure without sin, and every member of the same, through faith in Christ; and that they are in the full favour of God.[52]

The emphasis upon love for God's law certainly reflects Tyndale's concept of the didactic use of the law in the Christian life. Like Barnes, he saw the corporate good works of believers as one more sign of the true Church.

The priesthood of the true Church was also an ecclesiological aspect in which William Tyndale was intently interested. His advocacy of the universal priesthood of believers is another evidence of his essential community with Luther.[53]

Because of his concept of the priesthood of believers, Tyndale objected strongly to the Catholic view of the clergy. He insisted that the New Testament word *presbyteros* signified "elder," not priest. "An elder . . . is nothing but an officer to teach, and not . . . a mediator between God and us."[54] Consequently, there is no spiritual ministry which is the exclusive province of the clergy. Tyndale believed that the ministry of the Word and sacraments should be entrusted to a called and ordained pastor, but it is the congregation that calls and ordains him. If he proves unfaithful, the congregation may remove him.[55] Likewise, it is always appropriate for the ordinary Christian to minister the Word to his family, and to his acquaintances on a man-to-man basis.[56] Rather than require laymen to be in subjection to the clergy, Tyndale would make them proctors of the clergy. Not only did the medieval Church regard the clergy as sacramentally elevated to a position of piety and authority superior to the laity, it also recognized gradations within the clergy. Above the parish priest was the bishop as the executive authority over a diocese. Tyndale used his exegetical talents to expose the lack of a Biblical basis for such a position. Citing specific passages of the Greek New Testament, he showed that the terms *presbyteros* (elder) and *episcopos* (bishop) are used interchangeably in the Scripture.[57]

Although Master Tyndale was highly competent in composing linguistic-exegetical arguments to undermine the episcopacy, his attacks were rarely exressed in the dispassionate prose of a philologist. He was first and foremost a Protestant propagandist on a crusade against a religious establishment which he regarded as the principal agency of

Antichrist. Therefore, he assailed the entire Roman hierarchy, beginning with the pope.

In 1531, while a refugee in Antwerp, Tyndale wrote his *Exposition of the First Epistle of St. John.* This work contains a passage which relates its author's deep-seated hostility to the Roman papacy. It is worth quoting at length.

> Truly, . . . the bishop of Rome seeks himself, as all heretics did; and abuses the name of Christ, to gather offerings, tithes and rents in his name, to bestow them unto his own honor and not Christ's, and to bring the conscience of the people into captivity under him through superstitious fear, as though he had such authority given him of Christ. . . . And, with Pelagius, he preaches the justifying of works; which is the denying of Christ. He preaches a false binding and loosing with ear-confession, which is not in the trust and confidence of Christ's blood-shedding.[58]

In expressing his opinion of the prelates of England, Tyndale was not one wit more tactful. He labeled them "blind leaders of the blind; indurate and obstinate hypocrites."[59] Tyndale saw the pope as Antichrist and the prelates and priests as his agents. Tyndale could see no good whatever in the papal Church. To him it was "a terrible chimera, devouring the life of all religion and all thought; or a huge, pitiless machine, remorselessly pursuing its own purposes, reckless of the lives and happiness of those who stood in its onward path."[60]

Not only did William Tyndale assail the papal establishment as he knew it in the sixteenth century, but he also denied its historic claims to divine commission. His rejection of Petrine supremacy entailed the denial of the Roman teaching on apostolic succession and the doctrine of the keys.

The only apostolic succession which Tyndale would recognize was one of teaching. Those who teach the Apostles' doctrine are their successors, and historic connection or clerical ordination are irrelevant.[61] On the question of the keys, Tyndale, in line with Protestant thought in general, held that the Scriptures are the keys. "The Word of God truly preached does bind and loose the conscience."[62] That is, those who receive the Word in faith are loosed from their sins, and those who reject it are bound unto damnation. Those who declare the Word to effect the binding and loosing are simply instruments of God. Since the keys are the Scriptures, which have been committed to the whole Church, binding and loosing are the corporate ministry of the Church and not the exclusive sphere of the clergy.[63]

Tyndale was particularly incensed at what he regarded as a clerical perversion of the authority of the keys. He detested the Roman Catholic teaching that the pope and his agents could actually use the keys to permit or deny a person access to heaven, for example, by excommunication as practiced by the papists. Tyndale complained of the clergy:

> They take upon them greater authority than ever God gave them. For in their curses (as they call them) . . . they command God and Christ, and the angels, and all saints, to curse them: "Curse them God (they say), Father, Son, and Holy Spirit; curse them Virgin Mary," etc. O ye abominable! Who gave you authority to command God to curse? God commands you to bless, and you command him to curse![64]

According to Tyndale, the papal practice is inexcusable, for the New Testament supplies adequate illustration of how the keys are to be employed properly. The Apostles preached the Law and the Gospel. Let their would-be successors do likewise. Because he felt that the power of the keys was being generally abused, Tyndale warned his readers to beware of the priesthood's "counterfeit keys, and of their false net; which are their traditions and ceremonies, their hypocrisy and false doctrine, wherewith they catch, not souls unto Christ, but authority and riches unto themselves."[65]

Like Robert Barnes, William Tyndale did not advocate any specific pattern of church government, but he evinced no confidence that the existing ecclesiastical establishment could be persuaded to cooperate in the reform of the Church visible. Always, he insisted "on trying the present church by its fruits."[66] Tyndale would heartily join with Barnes when the latter asked, "he that will know which is the true Church of Christ, how shall he know it but by the scriptures only?"[67]

## THE SACRAMENTAL MINISTRY OF
## THE CHURCH

From the point of view of late medieval Catholicism, perhaps the most radical, and therefore the most abhorrent, feature of Protestantism was its rejection of the Church's approved sacramental theology. The formulators of that theology were the medieval scholastics, such as Hugo of St. Victor (d. 1141), Peter Lombard (d. 1160), Alexander of Hales (d. 1245), and Thomas Aquinas (d. 1274). The doctrine of the sacraments underwent a very slow evolution from ancient times, considerable diversity of opinion being evident as to both the nature and the number of such ordinances. It was Peter Lombard who succeeded in gaining broad acceptance for the seven sacraments which have become traditional in Roman Catholic practice. These seven — baptism, the Eucharist, confirmation, penance, extreme unction, holy orders, and matrimony — were finally accepted as official at a council of the Church in Florence, Italy in 1439. The official definition of the sacraments published in 1439 was largely that composed by Aquinas two centuries earlier.[68]

Although the objectives of the present study do not require an in-depth examination of medieval sacramentalism, one must understand something of the extreme importance attached to the sacraments by the late medieval Church in order to appreciate its sense of outrage at the Protestant challenge. As has been fittingly observed,

> All the lines of interest in medieval theology converge in the teaching concerning the sacraments. This teaching was conditioned by a two-fold interest: (1) the practical concern of the individual for some tangible form of salvation, and (2) the hierarchical tendencies of the age to bind the salvation of the individual to the Church. The sacraments became both a means of grace and a means to rule.[69]

Indeed, it would be quite accurate to conclude that it was *because* they were viewed as a means of grace, that the sacraments became a means to rule. Among the seven, baptism and penance were declared essential for absolution from sin, and the Eucharist, since the Fourth Lateran Council (1215), was officially regarded as conveying to the recipient the actual body and blood of Christ. The dispensation of the sacraments was virtually a monopoly of the priesthood. By means of excommunication and/or interdict, the Church possessed instruments of discipline, which, at times, had been highly effective in imposing its will upon recalcitrant laymen. Politically ambitious popes such as Gregory VII (d. 1085) and Innocent III (d. 1216) had used their powers of excommunication and interdict to effect the deposition of kings. Medieval man was often terrified at the prospect of being denied the sacraments, for he viewed them as the means of his salvation. If any sizable portion of Christendom were to be detached from this belief, the entire edifice of ecclesiastical power would be in jeopardy. This is precisely what happened in the Reformation.

## Martin Luther on the Sacraments

With Martin Luther again leading the way, the Protestant reformers of the sixteenth century collectively rejected the medieval theology of the sacraments. Not only did they reinterpret the significance of the sacraments, but they reduced the number to two — baptism and the Eucharist. Beyond their united rejection of the Roman position, however, the reformers never achieved agreement among themselves. The extent of their discord on the Eucharist became so great that, in 1577, Christopher Rasperger at Ingolstadt wrote a book entitled *Two Hundred Interpretations of the Words: This is my Body*.[70] The diversity of Protestant opinion notwithstanding, the existence and popularity of those opinions indicated that the medieval religious monolith had ceased to exist.

Luther raised the issue of the sacraments in his *Babylonian Captivity of the Church* (1520). There he categorically denied the sacramental character of all but baptism and the Eucharist, though he allowed the continuation of penance, or oral confession of sin, as a non-sacramental practice of spiritual value. He argued that sacramentalism, as practiced in the Roman Church, was the principal means whereby the papacy kept Christendom in bondage to its wishes.[71]

In his mature thought Luther taught that the sacraments are outward signs, instituted by Christ, connected with his divine word, and a means of conveying the forgiveness of sins. There can be no sacrament apart from the Word of God, and baptism and the Eucharist are the only ordinances which combine the outward sign with the promise of forgiveness.[72] Luther concurred with Augustine's description of the sacraments as the "visible word."

According to Luther, faith in the Word of God is essential to the sacraments. "There must be an unwavering, unshaken faith in the heart which receives the promise and sign and does not doubt that what God promises and signifies is indeed so."[73] In this way Luther argued against the Roman teaching that the sacraments, by virtue of their inherent efficacy, imparted grace to all except those who received them while in a state of mortal sin.

In addition to positing the promises of God (and faith in those promises) as essential to the sacraments, Luther held that one may be saved without the sacraments. It is faith in Christ that saves. "Faith is such a necessary part of the sacrament that it can save even without the sacrament."[74] Again, he said, "One can become righteous by faith without the bodily reception of the sacraments [so long as one does not despise them]."[75]

Since God instituted the sacraments and chooses to convey grace by means of them, man must not depreciate them as mere worthless external signs, as the spiritualists and some other radical sects of Luther's day were doing.

Highly illustrative of Luther's teaching on the relationship of faith to the sacraments is his explanation of baptism in his *Small Catechism*. There he declared that baptism "works forgiveness of sins, delivers from death and the devil, and confers everlasting salvation on all who believe, as the Word and promise of God declare." Quickly then, he raised the question: how can water accomplish such marvels? To this he replied:

> It is not the water indeed that produces these effects, but the Word of God which accompanies and is connected with the water, and our faith which relies on the Word of God connected with the water. For the water, without the Word of God, is simply water and no baptism.[76]

For the Christian, baptism signifies death and resurrection. It is a constant reminder to renew repentance by putting the "old man" to death, and daily rising to new spiritual life in Christ.[77] Luther saw the Christian experience as a life-long pursuit of the principle signified by baptism.[78]

Most of what Luther wrote on the sacraments was intended as polemic to combat views he found objectionable. In this connection, he fiercely defended the practice of infant baptism against the Anabaptists who insisted that belief in Christ is a prerequisite for baptism. They maintained that infants cannot believe and therefore must not be baptized.

Because of the earlier connection he had made between faith and the sacraments, Luther's defense of infant baptism required further explanation. The most compact presentation of his apology appeared in his *Large Catechism* (1529). There he argued that infant baptism has been the universal practice of the Church from antiquity. The weight of its catholicity is a crushing blow to the innovators who would abandon it.

Moreover, Luther rejected the Anabaptist tenet that infants cannot possess faith. Since faith is a gift from God, he may impart it when he will, even to infants! They may be incapable of conscious belief, but the faith given to them in infancy will appear in later life. To those who dismissed this as a presumption, Luther replied that no one is *ever* certain of another's faith. Therefore, even when a professing adult is baptized, it is still on the *presumption* that he has faith.[79]

In order to strengthen his rebuttal of the Anabaptists, Luther also qualified his earlier teaching on the relationship of faith to the sacraments. In the *Large Catechism* he asserted that lack of faith does not render baptism invalid, for "faith does not constitute baptism but receives it." Therefore, "we bring the child with the purpose and hope that he may believe, and we pray God to grant him faith."[80] Luther insisted that the lack of a specific New Testament command to baptize infants was no argument against the practice, for no one could cite a passage excluding infants from the sacrament. The burden of proof, therefore, is on the innovators. When the Church ministers baptism, it is obeying the command of Christ. If and when the sacrament is used wrongly, the abuse is a reflection upon the character of the offender and not upon the integrity of baptism.[81]

The second sacrament recognized by the reformers was the Eucharist, which Luther defined as "the true body and blood of our Lord Jesus Christ under the bread and wine, given unto us Christians to eat and drink, as it was instituted by Christ himself." As to the benefits conveyed by this sacrament, Luther said they are "the remission of sins, life, and salvation."[82]

Luther's great concern in setting forth his view of the Eucharist was to maintain belief in the Real Presence of Christ in the sacrament. Since the Fourth Lateran Council

(1215), the doctrine of the Real Presence under the concept of transubstantiation had been a dogma of the medieval Church. Transubstantiation is the teaching that the bread and wine of the Eucharist actually lose their substance as bread and wine and change into the body and blood of Christ when consecrated by a priest in the sacrifice of the mass.

Luther's belief in the death of Christ as the perfect and final atonement for sin necessitated his rejection of the mass as a sacrifice, but he retained his belief in the Real Presence, although not in the sense of transubstantiation. His controversial writings on the Eucharist show him contending against the Roman view on one side and the symbolic concept of Zwingli and the Anabaptists on the other. Luther's view (by some erroneously called "consubstantiation") was that the body and blood of Christ are truly present "in, with, and under" the bread and wine, though the substance of those elements remains unchanged.[83] By this, Luther was not trying to develop a new philosophical explanation of *how* the miracle takes place (as the term "consubstantion" would imply), but he was simply recasting and reasserting his conviction that Christ literally meant what he said with the words, "This *is* my body." Luther's belief in the Real Presence was so firm against those who saw mere symbols in the bread and wine that he exclaimed, "sooner than have mere wine with the fanatics, I would agree with the pope that there is only blood."[84]

On the point of how partaking of the sacrament conveys forgiveness, life, and salvation he wrote:

> The eating and drinking, indeed, do not produce them, but the words which stand here, namely: "Given and shed for you, for the remission of

sins." These words are, besides the bodily eating and drinking, the chief things in the sacrament: and he who believes these words, has that which they declare and set forth, namely, the remission of sins.[85]

As with baptism, man may be saved without the Eucharist, but not without the Word of God which it proclaims.[86]

Luther realized that his eucharistic position was incomprehensible to human reason, but to him that was of no consequence so long as he remained obedient to God's Word. His doctrine was established by a literal exegesis of the scripture passages in question, and he never retreated from it. Luther insisted that the sacrament is a gift from God which conveys the forgiveness of sins. It is a means of grace. It is the Gospel in action. Christ is really present there, and faith is strengthened by the grace which this sacrament imparts.

The blessed effects of the Eucharist, according to Luther, are imparted only to those who receive the sacrament in faith. It is "poison and death if it is eaten without faith and the Word."[87] In other words, the validity of the sacrament does not depend upon the state of the recipient. It is an objective gift from God bringing grace to the believer and declaring damnation to the unbeliever.

For Luther, the question of the sacraments was crucial to the whole reform, for it was inextricably involved in the key issues of salvation and the Church. The early English reformers likewise recognized the decisive importance of the sacramental question, and, consequently, they became doughty defenders of their respective interpretations.

161

## Robert Barnes on the Sacraments

On the matter of the Eucharist and the mass, Robert Barnes expressed his views in two specific treatises. On baptism and the other ordinances traditionally regarded as sacraments, however, he said very little.

From his final confession of faith at the stake, it is apparent that Barnes held to infant baptism, as a disciple of Luther would be expected to do. This, however, may only be surmised by implication. Moments before his death, Barnes publicly dissociated himself from the Anabaptists, excoriating them for their denial that Christ "did take any flesh of the Virgin Mary." Barnes referred to the Reformation radicals as "sects I detest and abhor."[88] This public repudiation of the Anabaptists, plus his overall adherence to Luther's theology and the absence of any disparagement of infant baptism in his writings, makes it appear certain that Barnes approved the practice.

Barnes' silence on the baptismal question until he went to the stake still leaves the modern reader somewhat confused. It is impossible to appraise any evolution of his thinking on the subject. At the point of martyrdom, he made the unqualified statement that baptism is "God's ordinance and is necessary for salvation."[89] Unfortunately, the complete absence of collateral evidence precludes making a judgment on the exact sense in which Barnes intended his remark to be understood. We will in this life probably never know anything concrete about Barnes' views on baptism.

Fortunately, Barnes has left us some materials which reflect aspects of his eucharistic beliefs. *Of the original of the Masse and of every part thereof* contains Barnes' attack upon the medieval concept of the mass as a re-enactment of the sacrifice of Christ on Calvary. In this work he specifically denied the tradition that the mass originated in Christ's command to the Apostle James. In the manner of a medieval chronicler, Barnes listed the various liturgical features of the mass together with the names of those responsible for instituting them and the dates of their introduction. His conclusion was that the papal claims are fraudulent, and that the origin of the mass cannot be traced earlier than 200 years after the Apostle James' death.[90]

Another feature of the eucharistic practice which became a matter of urgent concern for Robert Barnes was the question of giving the sacramental cup to the laity. Since transubstantiation had been made a dogma of faith in 1215, the practice gradually emerged of serving only the bread to the lay communicant lest the sacred contents of the chalice be desecrated by spilling. The Council of Constance (1415) made the withholding of the cup from the laity mandatory. Scholastic theologians taught that the whole presence of Christ was resident in the transubstantiated bread.[91]

Martin Luther set the tone of the reformers' protest against denying the cup to the laity in a treatise on *Receiving Both Kinds in the Sacrament.*[92] Robert Barnes eventually followed suit with his *That all men are bounde to receive the holy Communion under both kyndes under the payne of deadly sinne.* There Barnes assailed the conciliar decision at Constance, declaring that by its standard, Christ and the Apostle Paul would be branded heretics. As Barnes saw it, denial of the cup is a violation of the plain command of Christ to "drink all of it."[93] Only the servants of Antichrist deprive men of the cup of blessing. Speaking of the blood of Christ, Barnes asked, "was it not shed for laymen's sins? Why shall they not then drink of it?"[94]

Bishop John Fisher attempted to defend the traditional

practice by arguing that Christ's command to drink was directed only to the Apostles, not to ordinary laymen. Barnes retorted that canon law recognizes only the bishops and not ordinary priests as successors to the Apostles. Therefore, by Fisher's standard, only the bishops should partake of the cup.[95]

The main point of Barnes' argument was that denial of the cup is downright disobedience to a direct command of Christ. In order to add weight to his position, Barnes cited St. Cyprian (d. 248) and St. Ambrose (d. 397), Fathers of the Church who believed as he did.[96]

Barnes' convictions on the matter of the eucharistic cup were so strong that he felt constrained to appeal for the support of the king. He warned Henry VIII that the king would incur severe divine displeasure if he did not support a return to Biblical sacramental practice. He implored Henry not to be misled by the rationalizing circumlocutions of sophistical clerics. In his zeal for this cause, Barnes seemed to call the whole English nation to defend the ancient Biblical practice.

> I do exhort and require with all honour, yes and I do command in the virtue of Christ Jesus and his blessed word, all Dukes, all Earls, all Lords, all manner of estates high and low, . . . that they do see this ordinance of the God of heaven observed to the uttermost of their power. . . . It is no child's game to trifle with God's word. God will not be trifled with nor yet mocked.[97]

From the obvious fervor with which he pleaded for the layman's right to the eucharistic cup, one would expect Barnes to have defined his doctrine of the Eucharist fully and clearly. Such, however, was not the case. Instead, his statements on the nature of the sacrament are few, and what he did write is clouded by ambiguity. It is certain that he believed in the Real Presence, but it is difficult to tell the exact sense in which he believed Christ was present.[98]

That Barnes did not hold to a merely symbolic view of the Eucharist may be ascertained from three experiences of his career. In 1535, he was appointed to a commission entrusted with combatting the influence of Anabaptism.[99] In his capacity as a commissioner, he received a copy of a thesis of John Lambert in which the latter denied the Real Presence. Barnes urged Lambert to discuss his thesis with Archbishop Cranmer. The matter was finally taken to the king who ordered Lambert's execution for heresy. It is highly significant that the martyrologist Foxe, usually an enthusiast for Barnes, suggests that Barnes' intolerance toward the symbolic interpretation of the Eucharist may have been his reason for advising Lambert to walk a path which eventually led to the stake.

A second persuasive evidence that Barnes held to the Real Presence is his own declaration of the fact at his martyrdom. In his final protestation at the stake, Barnes, replying to a question from a Mr. Pope about the sacrament of the altar, said:

> After long reasoning and disputation I declared and said, that the sacrament being rightly used and according to scripture does, after the word spoken by the priest, change the substance of the bread and wine into the body and blood of Christ.[101]

It is difficult to construe this statement as anything other than an affirmation of transubstantiation. Nevertheless, there are other factors which must be given due consideration. After Barnes' death, Luther published a German edition of Barnes' confession of faith at the stake. To this *Bekantnus dess Glaubens,* Luther added a preface in which he profusely praised the English martyr, even citing him as "St. Robert."[102] Now the question must be raised whether Luther would be so laudatory toward one who espoused transubstantiation. Knowing how extremely critical Luther was toward those who disputed his doctrine of the Real Presence, it is almost inconceivable that he could have understood Barnes to be teaching transubstantiation as Rome taught it in connection with the sacrifice of the mass.

A third episode in Barnes' career further reflects the ambiguity of his eucharistic belief. Under the Act of Six Articles (1539) transubstantiation was declared the official belief of the English Church, and denial of that doctrine was punishable by death. One of the victims of the royal reaction against Protestantism was Robert Mekins, a 15-year-old boy accused of heresy on the question of the sacrament of the altar. Although the boy recanted, he was burned at Smithfield, for the Six Articles provided no clemency for abjured heretics.

What is most intriguing about this tragic incident is that young Mekins claimed that he had been instructed in a heretical view of the sacrament by Robert Barnes![103] If Mekins told the truth, it appears certain that Barnes did not espouse transubstantiation. On the basis of this evidence, one modern critic of the English Reformation concluded that Barnes held to consubstantiation and taught the same to Richard Mekins.[104] This is a logical possibility to be sure, but there is still nothing from Barnes' pen specifically affirming that view.

Finally, on this subject, the whole tenor of Barnes' theology seems to militate against any adherence to the traditional Roman Catholic teaching. One need only recall his concept of the universal priesthood of believers and the doctrine of the keys to see how utterly incompatible his thinking on these matters would be with transubstantiation. He deplored the idea of the priesthood holding special sacramental powers as the Catholic belief entailed. And his fellow reformer John Frith did not understand Barnes to be an adherent of transubstantiation. Thomas More attacked Frith for holding heretical views on the sacrament of the altar. In the quarrel, More actually cited Barnes as a believer in the Real Presence, using Barnes for debating leverage against Frith. Frith replied to this tactic by insisting that he had no serious dispute with Luther and Barnes, since "both agree with him that the sacrament was not to be worshiped; and that idolatry being taken away, he was content to permit every man to judge of the sacrament, as God would put into their hearts."[105]

In the light of the conflicting nature of available evidence, it appears that there is no way to ascertain Barnes' exact eucharistic position. It is definite that he did not hold a Zwinglian symbolic view, and, despite the language of his confession at the stake, it seems highly improbable that he subscribed to the Roman concept of transubstantiation. He believed in the Real Presence, but, in exactly what sense we cannot say.

By acknowledging baptism and the Eucharist as the only Scriptural sacraments, the reformers either openly rejected or simply ignored the other five such ordinances which held sacramental status in the medieval Church. Of the five, matrimony was the only one which seemed to be of great interest to Robert Barnes, and then mainly because of his opposition to compulsory celibacy for the clergy.

The practice of requiring the clergy to remain unmarried had a long history reaching back to the fourth century, but it had always been difficult to gain full compliance. By the sixteenth century, clerical marriages were still quite common despite the canon law prohibition. Erasmus, for example, was both the son of such a union and an advocate of canonically legalizing the practice.[106]

Barnes entered the controversy about clerical celibacy in 1534 with a treatise entitled *That by God's worde it is lawful for Priests that hath not the gift of chastitie to marry Wives.*

The first part of this treatise is an exposition of relevant scripture passages to defend the marriage of the clergy. Satisfied that the New Testament poses no hindrance to such marriages, Barnes moved on to extol the benefits of the married state. He did so completely without selfish motives, for he was unmarried himself.[107]

Robert Barnes felt that neither marriage nor celibacy was, *per se,* spiritually superior. One could serve God in either state, but the celibate life required that one possess the "gift of chastity" — a divine endowment which allows a person to live contentedly without sexual pleasure. The vast majority of people, however, do not possess this gift; so for those who cannot remain chaste, "there is no other remedy ordained by God to avoid fornication but marriage."[108] Indeed, if one does not have the gift of chastity, he is morally obligated to marry.

On the specific question of the clergy, Barnes complained that married priests were mercilessly persecuted all over Europe, while clerics who kept whores were given comfortable livings and positions of honor.[109] As Barnes put it, "virginity is no nearer way to heaven than marriage, . . . but a thing of itself by God's ordinance indifferent." Moreover, Barnes charged, by binding the clergy to celibacy, the pope was leading them into sin.[110] With biting sarcasm he asked: "The pope reckons it filthy . . . that a priest with holy hands touch a woman's body, and with the same hands to consecrate the holy sacrament. . . . Why are not your hands defiled for handling whore's flesh?"[111]

In the interest of strengthening his argument against enforced celibacy, Barnes cited patristic authors whom he believed supported his position. He cited Augustine, Ambrose and Jerome, concluding that Augustine even urged those who had taken vows of chastity but could not keep them, to marry.[112] It would seem that Barnes misread, or perhaps misused, these Fathers of the ancient Church. The greatest modern authority on the history of clerical celibacy credits the influence of Augustine, Ambrose, and Jerome with being responsible for the triumph of the pro-celibacy party in the Western Church.[113]

According to Robert Barnes, enforced celibacy has produced the most heinous evils, among them clerical concubinage and the murder of children illegitimately sired by priests. His conclusion was that the pope cared nothing about the chastity of his clergy, but was really interested in the fees collected from them for dispensations allowing them release from their vows.[114]

Although he did not regard marriage as a sacrament, Barnes did hold it in high esteem as a pure sexual relationship ordained by God as the norm for the preponderant majority of men and women. This reformer's attack upon compulsory celibacy for the clergy was only one more expression of his doctrine of the universal priesthood of believers. Barnes' arguments against clerical celibacy bear marked similarity to those of Martin Luther.[115]

## William Tyndale on the Sacraments

In his *Obedience of a Christian Man* Master William Tyndale expressed his convictions regarding the sacramental ministry of the Church. After a brief discussion of each of the seven ordinances customarily designated sacraments, he cited baptism and the Eucharist as being the only ones Scripturally enjoined. Tyndale defined a sacrament as a sign ordained by God representing a promise of God to forgive our sins. The sign must be accompanied by the Word of God, and the sacrament cannot be efficacious without the faith of the recipient trusting in the promise which the Word declares. The sacraments do not save men except in the sense that they are instruments which effect salvation through their proclamation of the Gospel.[116] Faith in Christ saves, even apart from the sacraments.[117]

Tyndale distinguished sharply between what he regarded as true and false sacraments. He held that the true sacraments "preach the faith of Christ, as his Apostles did, and thereby justify," while the signs and ceremonies of Antichrist are "dumb," that is, they do not proclaim God's Word. "Where no promise of God is, there can be no faith, nor justifying, nor forgiveness of sins."[118] Thus, the Roman ceremonies, which do not proclaim the forgiveness of sins through Christ's blood, are pseudo-sacraments. To Thomas More, Tyndale complained that the pope had perverted the sacraments and "robbed us of the true sense of all scripture."[119]

The sacrament of baptism Tyndale regarded as a purifying and cleansing washing to those who receive it by faith in Christ. He saw no miraculous power in the water itself, but the purifying comes through the word of God's promise, which the baptismal water portrays. "The washing preaches unto us, that we are cleansed with Christ's blood-shedding; which was an offering, and a satisfaction for the sin of all that repent and believe, consenting and submitting themselves unto the will of God."[120]

As for the precise symbolism of baptism, Tyndale cited St. Paul's Epistle to the Romans as teaching that death, burial, and resurrection are depicted. That is, baptism portrays the believer's death to the old life of sin as he is "buried" under the water, and his resurrection to new spiritual life in Christ as he rises from the water. It was Tyndale's opinion that baptism by total immersion best depicts this experience.[121]

As the Protestant reformers rejected the medieval Catholic teaching that the sacraments are efficacious *ex opere operato,* they were confronted with the problem of how to justify infant baptism if faith in the Word of God is essential to make the sacrament effectual. As already shown, Luther clarified his view of the sacrament as regards the baptism of infants.[122]

In his attempt to defend the practice of baptizing infants, Tyndale did not follow Luther's full line of argumentation. He did not appeal to the strength of tradition, nor did he speak about an "infant faith." His approach sought for the antecedent of Christian baptism in the Old Testament. Through exegesis of relevant scripture passages, Tyndale found that the Old Testament believers were given an outward sign of their covenant relationship to God in circumcision. In the book of Genesis, chapter 17, it is recorded that the Lord made a covenant promise to Abraham and his descendants to be their God and to bless them. Abraham and the men with him were to be circumcized, and every male child born into the covenantal nation was to be circumcised on the eighth day after birth. The benefits of the covenant included them, and therefore they were given the covenant sign of circumcision.

Turning to the New Testament (covenant), William Tyndale understood it to teach that the people of God are yet in a covenant relationship to their Lord, the sign of this covenant being baptism, the successor to circumcision. Christian parents are bound to receive this sacrament themselves, and to "put this sign upon our children," as the Israelites did under the Old Covenant. In so doing, parents bind themselves to bring their children "to the knowledge of God the Father, and of Christ, and of their duty to God and his law."[123] "Instead of circumcision came our baptism; whereby we are received into the religion of Christ, and made partakers of his passion, and members of his church."[124]

Although infants were to be baptized because of their covenant position, Tyndale asserted, "as the circumcised in the flesh, and not in the heart, have no part in God's good promises; even so they that are baptized in the flesh, and not in the heart, have no part in Christ's blood."[125] In other words, it is the covenant promise of God which brings salvation. As circumcision did not guarantee salvation under the Old Covenant, baptism does not assure it under the New. There must be a personal faith in Christ who is the executor of the covenant of redemption. Children of the covenant must confirm their baptism by individual commitment to Christ. The fact that they have been baptized should stir them to faith.[126] Apart from the Word of God received by faith "that outward washing, which is the visible sacrament or sign justifies us not."[127] Tyndale's method of defending infant baptism differed considerably from Luther's; as a result he was one step farther removed from Luther's baptismal view than was Barnes.

The nature and significance of the Eucharist was the second great sacramental matter debated between reformers and traditionalists, and among the reformers themselves. William Tyndale summarized his views on this subject in his undated treatise, *A Brief Declaration of the Sacraments,* though numerous other expressions of his views may be found in his expository and polemical works.

Tyndale saw the Eucharist as the most effective means to portray the death of Christ, and, thereby, nourish faith in the promises of the covenant of redemption. He saw it as a standing reminder of the merciful forgiveness of sins because of Christ's sacrifice. This sacrament is a gift *from* God, and not a service *to* God. That is, the Eucharist is a sacramental sign to man, but, in no sense, a sacrifice to God. Tyndale stood with Luther, Barnes and all the major reformers in absolutely rejecting the medieval concept of the Eucharist as a necessary re-enactment of Christ's sacrifice on the cross. Roman doctrine denied the all-sufficiency of Christ's atonement, so the reformers disavowed it vehemently.[128]

As he did with baptism, Tyndale sought the antecedent of the Eucharist in the Old Testament. In so doing, he strengthened his contention that it was not intended to be observed as a sacrifice.

The New Testament indicates that Jesus instituted the Eucharist on the last occasion when he celebrated the Passover meal with his disciples. The bread and wine now used in the Eucharist were originally traditional elements of the Passover *seder.* Tyndale concluded that the Eucharist of the New Covenant, therefore, is the successor to the *seder* of the Old Covenant. The Passover meal was clearly intended as a memorial to the redemption of the Israelites from their bondage in Egypt (Exodus 12). It was not a sacrifice by which that redemption had been effected. "The paschal lamb was a memorial of the deliverance out of Egypt only, and no satisfaction or offering for sin."[129] The New Covenant Eucharist is, likewise, a memorial and not a sacrifice.

> If a man say of the sacrament of Christ's body and blood, that it is a sacrifice as well for the dead as for the living, and therefore the very deed of itself justifies and puts away sin; I answer, that a sacrifice is the slaying of the body of a beast, or a man: wherefore, if it be a sacrifice, then is Christ's body there [on the altar of the mass] slain, and his blood shed; but that is not so. And therefore it is properly no sacrifice, but a sacrament, and a memorial of that everlasting sacrifice once for all, which he offered upon the cross.[130]

Having declared the Eucharist to be a sacramental memorial to Christ, Tyndale had to deal with the perplexing question of how to interpret Christ's words "this is my body, . . . this is my blood." Were these words of institution to be understood in a merely symbolical sense as held by Zwingli and the Swiss, or do they signify the Real Presence of Christ as taught by Luther and Barnes?

In a *Brief Declaration of the Sacraments* Tyndale surveyed the three major schools of eucharistic interpretation: Roman Catholic, Lutheran, and Reformed. For the reasons mentioned above, he rejected Catholic transubstantiation outright. Likewise, Tyndale apparently saw little real difference between the Catholic and Lutheran positions.[131] Specifically, he denied the contention that Christ's command requires a physical ingestion. To the contrary, Tyndale argued, "the righteous lives by his faith; *ergo,* to believe and trust in Christ's blood is the eating that there was meant, as the text well proves."[132]

After discussing the three schools of thought, William Tyndale referred to himself as being a holder of the Reformed opinion, using "Reformed" in the Zwinglian sense.[133] This self-disclosure, however, does not prove that he was a Zwinglian. Tyndale also considered the Eucharist as a means of grace to the believing recipient whereby his faith is strengthened. The sacrament makes faith "sink down into the heart."[134] It "stirs up our repenting faith, to call to mind the death and passion of Christ for our sins."[135] In thus viewing the sacrament as a means of grace, Tyndale went well beyond a simply symbolical interpretation.

Although he was not explicit on the question of Christ's presence in the Eucharist, it appears that Tyndale anticipated the idea of a spiritual presence of Christ soon to be enunciated by John Calvin,[136] while he forthrightly rejected transubstantiation.

Perhaps the reason one cannot find in Tyndale a specific espousal of any of the eucharistic views current in the early sixteenth century is due to a deliberate evasiveness. It is evident that he recognized this subject to be an extremely divisive element within the Evangelical camp. When he became aware that John Frith was advocating a symbolical interpretation, Tyndale wrote to him: "Of the presence of Christ's body in the sacrament, meddle as little as you can, that there appear no division among us. Barnes will be hot against you."[137] Tyndale knew that Barnes was contentious by nature, and that he would probably be incensed at any denial of the Real Presence, even from a fellow reformer.[138]

In concluding his discourse on the sacraments, Tyndale appealed for understanding among Christian brethren who might not be in complete agreement on the question of the eucharistic presence. So long as the sacrament was not used idolatrously, he saw no reason why fellowship should be impaired over this matter.[139] Tyndale's willingness to relegate the matter of the eucharistic presence to the periphery of theological discussion was, of course, quite un-Lutheran. Whereas Tyndale was anxious to accommodate differences of opinion on this matter for the sake of Protestant unity, Luther resolutely refused to compromise with Zwingli on this question at a time when the threat of imperial action against the reformers seemed to make evangelical unity a necessity for the survival of the cause. Here is evidence that Tyndale's most significant difference with Luther was not only the nature of the eucharistic presence, but also the matter of just how important the doctrine was to the Christian faith itself.

Like Robert Barnes, William Tyndale wrote about marriage, though he never married. Also like Barnes, his chief interest in the subject was to attack the Catholic insistence on clerical celibacy. Tyndale did not compose a separate treatise on matrimony vs. celibacy as Barnes did, but he largely expressed the same ideas in his occasional writings.

In a brief subsection of *The Obedience of a Christian Man,* Tyndale discussed whether matrimony should be regarded as a sacrament. Because this ordinance contains no promise comparable to the forgiveness of sins promised in baptism and the Eucharist, he concluded "it ought not to be called a sacrament."[140]

A major point in Tyndale's opposition to compulsory clerical celibacy was his belief that it belittled the sanctity of marriage while encouraging immorality among the clergy. Citing episodes narrated in medieval chronicles, Tyndale charged: "When the holy father had forbidden priests their wives, the bishops permitted them whores of their own, for a yearly tribute; and do still in all lands save in England, where they may not have any other save men's wives only."[141]

Not only did Master Tyndale assail enforced celibacy, but he argued that, in most cases, marriage is an asset to a cleric. He saw the experience of a man ruling his family as excellent training for the responsibilities of the ministry. Likewise, Tyndale held that having a wife would aid a cleric in overcoming the temptation to immorality since "chastity is an exceeding seldom gift."[142] Apparently, Tyndale and Barnes both felt that they were among the few endowed with this gift. Because so few possess the gift of chastity, William Tyndale strongly discouraged the assuming of vows of celibacy. He felt that careless adoption of such vows was responsible for the homosexuality, which he believed was also rampant among the Roman clergy.[143]

Despite their community of thinking on the question of marriage vs. celibacy, Tyndale and Barnes held diametrically opposite views on the related subject of divorce, or, at least, as far as Henry VIII's case for a divorce from Catherine of Aragon was concerned. Tyndale stood alone among the early English reformers in opposing the royal divorce, while Barnes worked energetically on the Continent to solicit a favorable opinion from the Lutheran theologians.

In 1530 Tyndale wrote his *Practice of Prelates*, the most bitterly polemical of all his works. The reason for this writing was revealed in the subtitle, "Whether the king's grace may be separated from his queen." Actually, the subject of the royal divorce is a minor theme in this anticlerical tirade, in which Tyndale has been described as giving "full vent to the accumulated indignation of half a lifetime, and his words fall upon the reader with the terrible emphasis of the denunciations of the Hebrew prophets."[144]

In issuing his opinion on the divorce, Tyndale rejected the almost unanimous opinion of the English reformers that no lawful marriage existed because of the impediment of marriage to a brother's widow. According to Tyndale, Henry's marriage was right and lawful from the start, and no grounds existed to dissolve it.[145]

In William Tyndale's concept of the sacraments he diverged most sharply from Luther. He accepted baptism and the Eucharist as the only Scriptural sacraments — a conviction held in common with all the major reformers. Likewise, he held to infant baptism. Tyndale's method of justifying infant baptism, however, was more akin to that of Zwingli than Luther.[146] On the Eucharist Tyndale clearly rejected any concept of a physical presence, either by transubstantiation or consubstantiation, and he did not stand squarely on Luther's doctrine of the Real Presence. It appears that Tyndale's theology of the sacraments had much in common with the position of John Calvin. To give Tyndale's inventiveness due recognition, it should be noted that he died before Calvin's theological works were published.

CHAPTER 7

# THE QUESTION OF THE STATE

## LUTHER'S LEGACY

Writing in 1886, Robert Demaus, one of Tyndale's major biographers, incisively observed:

> The supremacy of Holy Scripture in all matters of faith, the supremacy of the civil law in all matters of discipline, such were the remedies which Tyndale recommended to his countrymen as the only effectual means of redressing the intolerable grievances under which they were groaning; and these are, in fact, the two pillars on which the Reformation in England was subsequently established.[1]

Second only to their overriding concern to try all spiritual and doctrinal matters by the supreme authority of the Bible, was the reformers' fervent advocacy of obedience to the lawful civil authority. Although they were branded heretics by their king, Robert Barnes and William Tyndale, in their generation, were among the foremost champions of the royal supremacy. In life and death they professed unswerving loyalty to Henry VIII, and, by their writings, they tried to inculcate the same loyalty in their readers.

Obviously, there were certain pragmatic considerations which moved these reformers to declare themselves so forcefully on their king's behalf. They knew that the horrors of the War of the Roses were still fresh in the memories of

Englishmen, and they realized that the Peasants' War in Germany had given the Reformation a subversive political image. Also, the reformers viewed the king as the best defense against foreign attack from the Holy Roman Emperor and the pope.

Barnes, Tyndale, and others made vigorous attempts to gain Henry's good will, and, hopefully, his conversion to the Evangelical faith. The practical advantages for themselves and their movement, which the reformers might have obtained from the king, are, of course, obvious. Still, their largely unsolicited support for the royal authority did have a definite religious motive. Indeed, it was based upon a theology of the state derived from their study of the Bible, and from the influence of Martin Luther.

In 1523 Luther published a treatise entitled *Temporal Authority: to what Extent it Should be Obeyed.* In this work he outlined his understanding of the Christian's relationship and responsibility to the civil government. Since Luther's theology of the state so strongly influenced his English disciples, it is necessary to summarize his doctrine as a background against which the thought of Barnes and Tyndale may be studied.

From his study of church history, Luther knew that the papacy often used the civil powers to further its designs. Especially had this been the case in the Church's dealings with deviant religious sects, as the Inquisition bears grim testimony. In Luther's own day, there was the imminent possibility that the Catholic Holy Roman Emperor would move to crush the Reformation by force. Some Catholic civil authorities had already begun ordering the destruction of Evangelical books at the time that Luther was writing his treatise on civil authority.[2]

In approaching the matter of obedience to civil authority, Luther enunciated his doctrine of the "two kingdoms." The doctrine was intended to cover church-state relations and the position of the Christian in his dual capacity as a citizen of the kingdom of Christ and a citizen of the earthly state.

Luther said: "We must provide a sound basis for the civil law and sword so no one will doubt that it is in the world by God's will and ordinance." He then cited as his authority the statement of the Apostle Paul: "Let every soul be subject to the governing authority for there is no authority except from God; the authority which everywhere exists has been ordained by God. He then who resists the governing authority resists the ordinance of God, . . . and . . . will incur judgment" (Romans 13:1-2).[3] From his study of this and parallel New Testament passages, Luther concluded, "It is God's will that the temporal sword and law be used for the punishment of the wicked and the protection of the upright."[4]

Anyone at all familiar with the New Testament will recognize that the severe treatment of evildoers prescribed by Romans 13 is not all that the Christian Scriptures have to say on the subject. There are other passages which speak in the opposite way. For example, "Love your enemies, do good to them that hate you" (Matthew 5:44). Many in Luther's day, and since, have expressed confusion at this seeming contradiction. Luther saw the solution to the dilemma in his "two kingdoms" concept.

All mankind, according to Luther's scheme, is divided into two classes: those belonging to the kingdom of God and those belonging to the kingdom of the world. The citizens of the first are all true Christians — believers of the Gospel, who are subject to the lordship of Christ. These do not need a temporal law enforced with the sword, and, if all men were true Christians, civil authority would not be necessary.

All men are not genuine Christians, however, and those who are not belong to the kingdom of the world, where the rule of law must prevail. In this kingdom the civil authority is ordained to restrain and punish evil so that they who "practice it . . . cannot do so without fear or with impunity."[5]

Both kingdoms (governments) are necessary, and God rules in both. The gospel is supreme in the first kingdom, and there human relations are regulated by love. In the second kingdom the law is supreme, and there God rules through civil authorities as his instruments of restraint and punishment of evildoers. The Christian lives in *both* kingdoms, and, because he needs the benefits of a civil society, the Christian must firmly support the temporal authorities in the execution of their divinely appointed task. In doing so, the Christian also promotes the welfare of his neighbors. Luther admonished all Christians:

> In what concerns you and yours, you govern yourself by the gospel and suffer injustice toward yourself as a true Christian; in what concerns the person or property of others, you govern yourself according to love and tolerate no injustice toward your neighbor. The gospel does not forbid this; . . . it actually commands it.[6]

One of the most effective ways that the Christian may serve God and his neighbor, Luther taught, was for the Christian to hold a position in the state government, "for those who punish evil and protect the good are God's servants and workmen."[7]

As a citizen of the earthly kingdom then, the Christian is obligated to obey the civil rulers and to co-operate with them in their lawful responsibilities. By this Luther, nevertheless, did not intend to award the temporal authorities unlimited powers of regulation over the lives of their subjects. On the contrary, he explicitly taught that there are limits both to the authority of rulers and to the obedience of subjects. The prince, or civil ruler, is sovereign within the sphere alloted him by God. That sphere encompasses only external things and does not embrace the realm of faith or the spirit. "A human ordinance cannot . . . extend its authority into heaven and over souls; it is limited to earth, to external things men have with one another, where they can see, know, judge, evaluate, punish, and acquit."[8]

At the time of Luther's writing *Temporal Authority* (1523), some of the German princes were vigorously opposing the Reformation, issuing laws to stop the spread of Evangelical teachings. Luther urged his readers to refuse compliance with such laws, for in issuing them the princes were overstepping the bounds of their sphere of authority and, thereby, becoming tyrants. In support of his advice, Luther quoted the Apostle Peter, "We must obey God rather than men" (Acts 5:29).

The nature of the civil disobedience which Luther advised in the above circumstances was that of passive resistance only, and not rebellion. He warned Christians to expect oppression when they take such a position and to suffer patiently, grateful for the privilege of suffering for Christ's sake. Oppressed believers must leave the offending prince to the justice of God.[9]

One group of contemporary officials which Luther felt were notoriously guilty of exceeding their sphere of authority were the bishops. He roundly criticized them for holding civil positions in which they behaved like worldly princes and neglected the care of souls — a charge echoed many times by the English reformers. Church and state have separate functions, and the bishops' role is to be servants of the Church, not rulers of the state.[10] Luther saw Church and state as separate institutions ordained by God to serve his purpose in the world. While remaining independent of each other, each should support the other in the execution, but not in the legislation, of its lawful responsibilities.

## ROBERT BARNES ON THE STATE

In his *Supplication unto the most gracious Prince Henry VIII*, first published in 1531, Barnes wrote to declare his own loyalty, and to combat the charge that Protestantism, by its very nature, was subversive. A short time earlier, a tract had appeared stating that some of the revolutionary disciples of John of Leyden, the Dutch Anabaptist, intended to migrate to England.[11] Enemies of the Reformation made propaganda of such material, so Barnes moved vigorously to thwart them. His defense was largely an offense against his clerical adversaries. He tried to convince Henry VIII that current clerical activities were subversive, and that subversion was a clerical tradition.

Barnes cited the reign of Gregory III (731-41), when the pope deposed Byzantine Emperor Leo III, as the beginning of papal intrusion into the political realm. Barnes held that this move was buttressed by a papal alliance with Charles Martel, which established France as Rome's chief agency to support papal political designs. Since France was England's traditional rival, Barnes' argument had a certain appeal. Furthermore, Barnes pointed to the struggle against separate ecclesiastical courts in England during the reign of King Henry II (1154-89), an issue still being debated at the time of his writing the *Supplication*. He likewise argued that the clergy opposed the circulation of a vernacular Bible because it would reveal their failure to obey and support the king as the Scriptures command.[12]

Like Martin Luther, Robert Barnes saw the civil government as a divinely ordained institution to which all citizens owe obedience. The government derives its authority directly from God, as Romans 13 teaches, and not by delegation from Rome, as the papacy had been teaching.[13] Barnes

Henry VIII, King of England

urged the king to realize that subversion of the state was the product of the papal argument that the "seat of Rome gives strength and might to all laws, but it is subject to none."[14] On the other hand, the reformers have never urged citizens to rebel. Rather, "they have been ready to lay down their own heads, to suffer with patience, whatsoever tyranny any power would minister to them, giving all people example to do the same."[15] Moreover, Evangelical theologians have insisted that the civil government is supreme in all temporal matters over clergy and laity alike.[16]

Reflecting on claims of the medieval papacy to supreme temporal as well as spiritual jurisdiction, Barnes flatly denied that the pope had the right to depose princes, even wicked and tyrannical princes. Barnes understood the Scriptures to command obedience to rulers, be they benevolent or despotic. He reminded his readers that John the Baptist submitted to evil King Herod, and Christ to Pontius Pilate. Therefore, Christ and the Apostles refute the papal claims.[17] In utter disgust with the Roman argument, Barnes asked: "How is it possible to invent a more pestilent doctrine than this is? Here is God's ruler despised, and hereby is open treason maintained."[18] Barnes insisted that his advocacy of the royal supremacy was the reason the clerics charged him with heresy.

In addition to urging civil obedience to the prince, Martin Luther became a forthright critic of princes who abused their power. In his *Treatise on Temporal Authority,* he even offered advice on how a prince could rule wisely.[19] Again, Robert Barnes followed his German tutor. Barnes' position was that the Christian clergy should rebuke evil or immoral rulers with the Word of God only and never seek to depose the prince. "The holy Church of God has no sword, but the spiritual sword, with which she does not kill, but make alive."[20]

One of Barnes' major complaints against the English episcopacy was that the bishops swore an oath of allegiance to the pope which, he said, made it impossible for them to be loyal to their king. Barnes pointedly accused the bishops of espionage for the pope, to whom they swore a "shameful, traitorous oath." Definitely, Barnes asked the prelates, "What do you mean that you swear only to the holy Church of Rome? Will you be traitors to . . . the holy Church of England?" In self-defense Barnes exclaimed, "I must be accused of treason. And why? Because you are sworn to the pope, and I am true to the king."[21]

Actually, Barnes' assault on the episcopal establishment was not intended to say that the episcopacy was evil *per se*. While he had expressed that sentiment in the 1531 edition of his *Supplication,* in the version of 1534 he simply argued that the bishops were evil only to the extent that they supported the political pretensions of Rome or promoted false doctrine. By 1534 Henry VIII had rejected papal authority, so Barnes modified his view to make it more attractive to the king. By this time Barnes was "advocating a national church subservient to its prince as the specific fulfillment of the New Testament pattern for church and state relations."[22] This idea seems to have arisen out of the circumstances, rather than from any influence of Luther. Barnes closed his *Supplication* with a personal plea for the king to judge between the bishops and himself, "which of us is truest and most faithful to God and your grace."[23]

In the 1531 edition of his *Supplication* Barnes had included a section entitled "That men's constitutions, which are not grounded in Scripture, bynde not the conscience of man under the payne of deadly sinne." Here Barnes mainly espoused Luther's concept of the distinct functions of church and state. He limited the authority of the king to the temporal realm, forbade rebellion and called for patient suffering under a tyranny. Should the king prohibit the circulation of the Scriptures, Barnes called Christians to disobey passively and suffer the wrath of the ruler, or, as a last resort, flee from the kingdom. "Sodom and Gomorrah shall be more lightly handled, than such princes that do persecute the holy Word of God," Barnes concluded.[24]

In the above essay, Robert Barnes reproduced Luther's concept of the two kingdoms idea-for-idea, if not word-for-word. In the 1534 revision of the *Supplication,* however, this essay was simply omitted. Under the changed conditions of 1534, Barnes would still hold that clerics have no legitimate temporal authority, but, to please the crown, he made no reference to limitations upon royal authority in the spiritual realm.[25] No doubt, Barnes looked to the king as the best hope for reforming the English Church, since the Church was impotent to reform itself. Perhaps this explains his extreme reverence for princely authority.

In his original writing on the subject of civil obedience (1531), Robert Barnes justified a subject's right to escape detention if his prince had arrested him for proclaiming God's Word. The single limitation he placed on this right was that one's escape must not provoke sedition. This was clearly an attempt to justify his own flight from England in 1529.[26] Barnes' final expression on the question of civil obedience, however, was a call for abject submission. At the stake he admonished the spectators:

I have been reported a preacher of sedition and disobedience to the king's majesty: but here I say

to you, that you are all bound by the commandment of God to obey your prince with all humility
and with all your heart, yes, not so much as in a
look to show yourselves disobedient unto him; and
that not only for fear of the sword, but also for
conscience sake before God. . . . Yes, and I say further, if the king should command you anything
against God's law, if it be in your power to resist
him, yet may you not do it.[27]

Even in death, Dr. Barnes extolled the authority of the
king. Apparently, Barnes felt that Henry's break with
Rome had removed one huge barrier to the reformation of
the English Church. Therefore, he died in the optimism that
the crown was still the best hope for the future. As Barnes
put it, "I beseech you all, to pray for the king's grace, . . .
that God may give him prosperity, and that he may long
reign among you; and after him that godly prince Edward
may so reign, that he may finish those things that his father
has begun."[28]

In his later thought, Robert Barnes diverged from the
theology of the state which he had learned from Luther. By
his martyrdom Barnes testified that he did not regard the
king as lord of his conscience, for at the stake this reformer
stalwartly affirmed his faith in the Evangelical doctrines
despite the king's disapproval of them. Barnes' death itself
was a dramatic protest against Henry's religious policy.
Nevertheless, probably no other early English reformer was
more supportive of the royal position. Clearly, Barnes believed that the king had every right to determine religious
policy, but he regretted that Henry had not yet been persuaded to make that policy the one urged upon him by the
reformers. Barnes was very much a patriot-reformer.

## WILLIAM TYNDALE ON THE STATE

Like Robert Barnes, William Tyndale spent much of his career as a religious refugee on the Continent. Also like Barnes, Tyndale's published advocacy of the Reformation incurred the charges of heresy and sedition. Judged by the standard of medieval orthodoxy, both reformers were doctrinally heretical, but, judged by their preaching and practice, neither was seditious.

Tyndale was perhaps the most articulate spokesman for Luther's doctrine of the two kingdoms and its concomitant view of civil obedience in the early English Reformation. Tyndale called the kingdom of God the "regiment of the gospel," and the kingdom of this world the "temporal regiment." In the first kingdom he saw all men as equals, "all alike good, all brethren, and Christ only is lord over all. Neither is there any other thing to do, or other law, except to love one another as Christ loved us."[29] In the temporal regiment (kingdom), however, there are necessary levels of authority, laws for the regulation of life, and means to enforce them. True Christians comprise the citizenry of the regiment of the gospel, but all men, believers and unbelievers alike, are citizens of the temporal regiment.

In his relationships as a citizen of God's kingdom, Tyndale taught, the Christian must be guided by his personal application of Christ's doctrine. In these relationships, therefore, there is no place for anger, hatred, revenge, etc. The believer must display humble patience in suffering whenever he is wronged, praying for and forgiving his enemies.

The relationships of the temporal kingdom, as Tyndale saw them, are quite different from those of the spiritual kingdom of God. In the kingdom of this world most men are not true Christians, and therefore will not relate to each other on the basis of love. Consequently government has been ordained by God to restrain and punish those who refuse to abide by the rule of law. Christians have a responsibility to support the civil authorities in law enforcement, and they should serve in civil positions when requested to do so. When a Christian serves in a position of civil authority, he must be motivated by love for his subjects; however, he may and must use necessary force to gain compliance with the law. In language reminiscent of Luther's tirade against the insurrectionary German peasants, Tyndale urged the civil authorities: "Those that are evil doers . . . and vex their brethren, and will not recognize you for their judge and fear your law, them smite, and draw upon them your sword, and put it not up until you have done your office."[30] In urging the obedience of his readers, Tyndale told them that they were obligated to obey their prince even in the matter of going to war on his behalf.[31]

The fervor with which William Tyndale promoted the concept of civil obedience reflects the strength of his conviction that temporal authority is of divine origin. Tyndale held that the civil laws "are the laws of God, and drawn out of the Ten Commandments and the natural law."[32] When a people flagrantly disobey the laws, God sometimes sends tyrants to govern them. Christ obeyed the civil law and taught his followers to do likewise.

In his exposition of the Sermon on the Mount, from which the above teachings are taken, Tyndale argued forcefully that the king's position is sacrosanct, for "the authority of the king is the authority of God."[33] Obviously, Tyndale did not mean this in an unqualified sense. He fully recognized that the king may abuse his power and reign wickedly. Should the king wrong his subjects, they "must complain to

God only." When subjects suffer under an unjust prince, they should examine themselves to discover for what sin God has sent the judgment of an oppressive ruler upon them.[34]

According to Tyndale, the only king who possesses absolute authority is God himself. Earthly princes rule only by authority delegated from heaven. In their standing before God, rulers and subjects are equal. The Word of God is superior to all temporal kings, and the lowest subject armed with the Word may admonish a king who violates God's Word. A man's body and goods are bound under the king's authority, but the Word is ever free. With it, a subject may warn a monarch who rules unjustly of the wrath of God to which he is liable.[35] The king rules in temporal affairs, but he is himself subject to the divine law.

Since the ruler's authority is not absolute, at what point, and in what ways is a Christian subject warranted in disobedience? This was a question with which every Protestant thinker had to deal. Tyndale's answer was typical of the reformers. He held simply that the Christian must obey his prince in all matters, except where the prince might require something which violates the laws of God. When necessity requires disobedience, it must be rendered passively and not rebelliously.

> God has made the king in every realm judge over all, and over him there is no judge. He that judges the king judges God; and he that lays hands on the king lays hands on God; and he that resists the king resists God, and damns God's law and ordinance.[36]

Tyndale believed that England had already suffered the divine wrath because men had attacked the person of the king. He deplored the murder of Richard II (1399) and concluded that the great reduction in the numbers of the nobility and the economic hardships of ensuing years were the products of the divine displeasure with those who "slew their right king whom God had anointed over them."[37]

In 1528 William Tyndale published his *Obedience of a Christian Man,* "wherein with singular dexterity, he instructs all men in the office and duty of Christian obedience,"[38] as the martyrologist Foxe put it. More recent interpreters have also been impressed with Tyndale's book. One referred to it as "a magazine from which subsequent reformers took most of their explosive doctrines."[39] Another concluded that Henry VIII was so impressed with *The Obedience* that its influence "may be traced in every act of parliament that led up to the royal supremacy."[40] Archbishop Warham reported that his scholars had found thirty heresies in this work. It was, nevertheless, the most popular of Tyndale's books with the exception of his New Testament.[41]

*The Obedience of a Christian Man* is deeply imbued with Luther's thinking, especially that expounded by the German reformer in *Temporal Authority: to what Extent it Should be Obeyed.*[42] Tyndale had been in Wittenberg on the eve of the Peasants' War, and his impressions are reflected in *The Obedience.* He completely shared Luther's concern for the maintenance of civil order.[43]

Tyndale's *Obedience* was a forthright reply to the Catholic charge that the Evangelical faith was subversive. In the same manner of attack to be used by Robert Barnes three years later, William Tyndale assailed his clerical opponents as the real source of subversion in the kingdom. In fact, it seems that Barnes' *Supplication* was at least partially inspired by his reading of Tyndale's *Obedience.*

The first point that Tyndale made in his prologue was to

brand England's prelates as subversive.[44] He soon followed
this with the charge that monastic vows were a subterfuge
to evade obedience to parental and civil authority.[45]

Although Tyndale believed civil government to be essential for the restraint and punishment of evildoers, he did not
hold that the prince was merely a necessary coercive force
to be endured. On the contrary, he maintained that obedience to temporal laws brings temporal benefits in the way
of a peaceful society in which prosperity may develop. He insisted that even an evil king is beneficial, for he will still
police the realm to protect it from criminals. Indeed, Tyndale concluded that God so carefully supervised the place-
ment of kings, that the nation received the kind of ruler it
deserved.[46]

In pursuing his attack on clericalism, Tyndale argued for
a church-state relationship consonant with his understanding of Luther's doctrine of the two kingdoms. He regarded
the papacy as an international instigator of strife among
states to further its own political ambitions. Therefore Tyndale urged his king scrupulously to avoid becoming a papal
pawn — advice which Henry enjoyed, but hardly needed.
Tyndale's point was that princes are ordained to punish
evil, not to fight the battles of the Roman Antichrist.[47]

With Barnes, Tyndale saw the English bishops as the major roadblock to the progress of reform, so he attacked them
furiously, insisting that their sphere of activity was rightly
religious and not political. Specifically, he called for the removal of prelates from all positions of civil responsibility.

> Let kings take their duty of their subjects, and
> that which is necessary to the defense of the
> realm. Let them rule their realms themselves,
> with the help of laymen that are sage, wise,

> learned and expert. Is it not a shame above all
> shames, and a monstrous thing, that no man
> should be found able to govern a worldly kingdom,
> save bishops and prelates; that ... are ... appoint-
> ed to preach the kingdom of God?[48]

As Tyndale read the records of the kingdom, politically-minded prelates had a shameful reputation for being manipulators of kings. Furthermore, he blamed their pernicious influence for the failure of the king to embrace the Gospel.[49] In no uncertain terms, Tyndale charged the bishops with disloyalty and deceit. "Though they pretend outwardly the honour of God or a commonwealth, their intent and secret counsel is only to bring all under their power, and to take out of the way whosoever hinders them, or is too mighty for them."[50] On seeking to satisfy their lust for power, the prelates, in Tyndale's estimation, were showing themselves to be apt pupils of their tutor the pope. Tyndale contended that all papal claims to temporal supremacy lacked scriptural foundations, and, therefore, were bogus. The pope has no temporal authority over any king and no jurisdiction over other bishops.[51]

Both Barnes and Tyndale regarded the existence of a separate system of ecclesiastical courts as incompatible with the sovereignty of the king and the independence of England. They called for the implementation of a single national law to which all citizens would be subject and a single system of courts where all offenders, clerical as well as lay, would be tried. As Tyndale expressed it, "one king, one law, is God's ordinance in every realm,"[52] and one need only look into the chronicles to see the ugly manifestations of clerical arrogance. He pointed particularly to the reign of King John (1199-1216) who was compelled to compromise himself and the nation by acknowledging Pope Innocent III as his feudal lord.[53] As a recent interpreter suggests:

> Out of the figure of King John, Tyndale created
> the basis for the first "Protestant" hero or martyr,
> one who sought to resist the tyranny of the pope
> for righteousness' sake and who was finally forced
> to yield to superior power.[54]

Not only did Tyndale defend the royal authority against clerical encroachments, but he also defended his fellow reformers accused of sedition by the clerics. He was especially energetic in his effort to vindicate Martin Luther, and, in so doing, Tyndale, as always, concluded that the real agitators of civil strife were the corrupt, politically-minded clerics.[55] "Here, Tyndale maintained, was the true fountain of insubordination and rebellion; here were the true apostles of sedition against whom the terror of the civil authority should be wielded."[56]

*The Obedience of a Christian Man* came to the attention of Henry VIII about the time that he was considering the removal of Thomas Cardinal Wolsey as chief minister. After Wolsey, laymen were made the royal ministers. Apparently, Henry found the anticlerical arguments of the reformers useful as he tried to justify his break with Rome.[57] After reading *The Obedience,* no one could honestly accuse its author of seditious Anabaptist tendencies.[58]

Although the reformers generally held that church and state had divinely ordered, but distinct, spheres of operation, they did not advocate a total separation of church and state. The idea of a secular society with a religiously neutral government was inconceivable to them. They did not want clerics to rule the state, nor civil authorities to govern in the realm of faith. Still, they envisioned as the ideal pattern a situation wherein church and state could cooperate under the benevolence of a truly Christian prince. For this reason, the reformers supported the national monarch against the international papacy.[59] In *The Obedience* Tyndale portrayed his image of the ideal Christian prince:

> Let kings if they had rather be Christian in deed than so to be called, give themselves altogether to the wealth [welfare] of their realms after the example of Christ, remembering that the people are God's, and not theirs; yes, are Christ's inheritance and possession, bought with his blood. The most despised person in his realm is the king's brother, and fellow member with him in the kingdom of God and of Christ. Let him therefore not think himself too good to do them service, neither seek any other thing in them than a father seeks in his children, yes, than Christ sought in us.[60]

In the final analysis, it is evident that the concept of civil obedience advocated by Robert Barnes and William Tyndale was actually more conservative than that urged by Martin Luther. Barnes and Tyndale were inflexible in their rejection of violent resistance to the prince regardless of how oppressive he might become. As indicated, this was Luther's position also, as his *Treatise on Temporal Authority* reveals. Luther, however, later modified his view in a rather significant way.

By 1530, the Protestant states of Germany were facing a grave crisis. The Imperial Diet of Augsburg heard and rejected the Lutheran theology, and Emperor Charles V threatened to move against the Protestant states with force. Led mainly by Prince Philip of Hesse, a number of states formed the Smalkald League, a defensive alliance of

Evangelicals against the Catholic emperor. The apparent imminence of an imperial attack took the question of civil obedience out of the realm of academic disputation and put it into the arena of political reality. German jurists composed intricate legal arguments to justify armed resistance to the emperor, and Luther reluctantly gave his approval. Fortunately for Luther, the expected war did not erupt until after his death, but he was now on record as giving qualified and reluctant, nevertheless genuine, endorsement to the concept of violent resistance.[61]

When compared to the submissiveness consistently urged by his English disciples, Luther's changed position appears almost radical. But in reality it was not — since Luther considered the "powers that be" in the constitution of the Holy Roman Empire superior to the authority of the emperor. The emperor was elected to carry out the provisions of the constitution. Luther's reluctance in approving resistance lay in his uncertainty about the arguments of the jurists against the emperor. Like Barnes and Tyndale, Luther did not want to become guilty of resisting "the powers that be."

## CHAPTER 8

# CONCLUSION

Dr. Robert Barnes and Master William Tyndale should not be regarded as seminal theological thinkers. This is mainly so because they concentrated on mediating to their countrymen the doctrinal teachings which they learned on the Continent. Both were humanists by training and methodology. Prior to their espousal of the Reformation, both were essentially Erasmian in their aspirations for ecclesiastical change. But under the impact of the Continental reformers, principally Luther, both became Protestant theologians.

Although a few recent interpreters have attempted to minimize Luther's influence on the thinking of Barnes and Tyndale, a careful contextual study of their writings has convinced the present writer that their debt to Luther was considerable. We have investigated the key subjects: authority, God and man, salvation, and church and state. In every case, the evidence of Luther's influence is undeniable.

To regard Barnes and Tyndale as transmitters of Luther's teachings to England, however, is not to make them mere mouthpieces for their German mentor. Both men did exercize independent judgment on theological questions. And on some points of doctrine, their conclusions varied from Luther's. This is especially apparent in their adherence to the didactic use of the divine law in the Christian life. Barnes' later thinking on church-state relations differed from Luther's, as did the sacramental theology of Tyndale. But the doctrines of *sola scriptura, sola gratia* and *sola fide* were the pillars of Lutheranism. Barnes and Tyndale embraced these principles, and from them they never wavered.

In appraising the enduring influence of Lutheran concepts in England, one must travel the paths first walked by Barnes and Tyndale. True, no English denomination of great size was to call itself the Lutheran Church, but the doctrinal content of Anglican theology bears unmistakable evidences of Lutheran teachings. A careful study of such documents as the *Ten Articles* (1536), the *Bishops' Book* (1537), and the *Thirteen Articles* (1538) supports this conclusion. Cranmer's *Book of Common Prayer* also borrowed heavily from Lutheran sources.[1]

In the second half of the sixteenth century, the tide of non-Lutheran Protestant influence from the Continent, especially from Switzerland and the Rhineland, rose significantly in England. Consequently, Zwinglian and Calvinistic religious ideas gained a large following during the reigns of Edward VI and Elizabeth I. The foundations of Anglican Protestantism, however, had been laid by an earlier generation of reformers, and prominent among them were the two men who represented Luther's English connection, Robert Barnes and William Tyndale.

# BIBLIOGRAPHY

## PRIMARY SOURCES

Augustine, Aurelius. *Later Works*. Edited by John Burnaby. Vol. VIII of the *Library of Christian Classics*. Philadelphia: 1955.

*Select Works of John Bale*. Edited by Henry Christmas for the Parker Society. Cambridge: 1849.

*The Reformation Essays of Dr. Robert Barnes*. Edited by Neelak S. Tjernagel. London: 1963.

Barnes, Robert. *Sententiae ex Doctoribus Collectae*. Wittenberg: 1530.

————. *Vitae Romanorum Pontificium*. Wittenberg: 1535.

*The Whole Works of W. Tyndall, John Frith, and Doct. Barnes*. London: 1573.

Becon, Thomas. *Prayers and other Pieces*. Edited by John Ayre for the Parker Society. Cambridge: 1844.

*Book of Concord*. Edited and translated by T. G. Tappert. Philadelphia: 1959.

*The Writings of John Bradford*. Edited by Aubrey Townsend for the Parker Society. Cambridge: 1848.

*Letters and Papers, Foreign and Domestic, of the Reign of Henry VIII*. 21 vols. Edited by John S. Brewer, *et. al.* London: 1862-1932.

Calvin, John. *Instruction in Faith*. Edited and translated by Paul T. Fuhrmann. Philadelphia: 1949.

————. *The Institutes of the Christian Religion*. 2 vols. Edited and translated by John Allen. Philadelphia: 1936.

*The Catechism of the Council of Trent*. Translated by J. Donovan. New York: 1829.

*Writings and Translations of Myles Coverdale*. 2 vols. Edited by George Pearson for the Parker Society. Cambridge: 1844 and 1846.

*Writings and Disputations of Thomas Cranmer*. Edited by John Cox for the Parker Society. Cambridge: 1844.

Ellis, Henry, ed. *Letters Illustrative of English History*. 3 vols. London: 1824.

*The Acts and Monuments of John Foxe*. 8 vols. New York: 1965.

Gardiner, Stephen. *Letters*. Edited by J. A. Muller. Cambridge: 1933.

Gardiner, Stephen. *Obedience in Church and State*. Edited by Pierre Janelle. London: 1930.

Great Britain Public Record Office. *Calendar of Letters, despatches, and state papers relating to the negotiations between England and Spain*. London: 1868.

Hall, Edward. *Henry VIII*. 2 vols. Edited by C. Whibley. London: 1904.

Harpsfield, Nicholas. *The Life and Death of Sir Thomas More, Knight.* London: 1932.

Herbert, Lord Edward of Cherbury. *Life and raigne of King Henry the Eighth.* London: 1649.

Hume, M. A. S., ed. and trans. *Chronicle of King Henry VIII of England written in Spanish by an unknown Hand.* London: 1889.

Joye, George. *An Apology made by George Joye to Satisfy W. Tyndall.* Edited by Edward Arber. Westminster: 1895.

*The Works of Hugh Latimer.* Edited by George E. Carrie for the Parker Society. 2 vols. Cambridge: 1845.

Luther, Martin. *Small Catechism.* Philadelphia: 1874.

*Luther's Works.* Edited by Helmut T. Lehmann and Jaroslav Pelikan. 56 vols. Philadelphia and St. Louis: 1957-1973.

More, Sir Thomas. *The Confutacyon of Tyndales Answere.* London: 1532.

*The Correspondence of Sir Thomas More.* Edited by Elizabeth Francis Rogers. Princeton: 1947.

*The Latin Epigrams of More.* Edited by Leicester Bradner and Charles A. Lynch. Chicago: 1953.

*St. Thomas More: Selected Letters.* Edited by Elizabeth Francis Rogers. New Haven: 1961.

Pocock, Nicholas, ed. *Records of the Reformation.* 2 vols. Oxford: 1870.

Pollard, A. W., ed. *Records of the English Bible.* London: 1911.

*The Works of Nicholas Ridley.* Edited by Henry Christmas for the Parker Society. 2 vols. Cambridge: 1841.

Robinson, Hastings, ed. *Original Letters Relative to the English Reformation.* Pt. 2. Cambridge: 1847.

Roger, William. *The Life of Sir Thomas More, Knyghte.* London: 1935.

Standish, John. *A Lyttle Treatise against the Protestation of Robert Barnes.* London: 1540.

Strype, John, ed. *Ecclesiastical Memorials Relating chiefly to Religion and the Reformation of it under King Henry VIII.* London: 1721.

————. *Memorials of Archbishop Cranmer.* 3 vols. Oxford: 1848-54.

Tyndale, William. *An Answer to Sir Thomas More's THE SUPPER OF THE LORD.* Edited by Henry Walter for the Parker Society. Cambridge: 1850.

————. *Doctrinal Treatises and Introductions to Different Portions of the Holy Scriptures.* Edited by Henry Walter for the Parker Society. Cambridge: 1848.

————. *Expositions and Notes on Sundry Portions of the Holy Scriptures together with the Practice of Prelates.* Edited by Henry Walter for the Parker Society. Cambridge: 1849.

Wriothesley, Charles. *A Chronicle of England during the Reigns of the Tudors.* 2 vols. Westminster: 1875-77.

Zwingli, Ulrich. "Of Baptism." *Zwingli and Bullinger.* Edited and translated by G. W. Bromiley. Vol. 24 of the *Library of Christian Classics.* Philadelphia: 1953.

# SECONDARY WORKS

Althaus, Paul. *The Theology of Martin Luther*. Translated by R. C. Schultz. Philadelphia: 1966.

Anderson, Charles S. "Robert Barnes on Luther," *Interpreters of Luther*. Edited by Jaroslav Pelikan. Philadelphia: 1968.

―――. "The Person and Position of Dr. Robert Barnes, 1495-1540: a Study in the Relationship between the English and German Reformations." Unpublished Th.D. dissertation, Union Theological Seminary, 1962.

Aston, Margaret. "Lollardy and the Reformation: Survival or Revival?" *History*, new series. Vol. 49 (June, 1964), pp. 149-170.

Atkinson, James. *Martin Luther and the Birth of Protestantism*. Baltimore: 1968.

Bainton, Roland H. *Early and Medieval Christianity*. Boston: 1962.

―――. *The Medieval Church*. Princeton: 1962.

Baumer, Franklin L. *Early Tudor Theory of Kingship*. New Haven: 1940.

Bornkamm, Heinrich. *Luther and the Old Testament*. Translated by E. W. and R. C. Gritsch. Philadelphia: 1969.

―――. *Luther's Doctrine of the Two Kingdoms*. Translated by Karl H. Hertz. Philadelphia: 1966.

Bridgett, T. E. *Life and Writing of Sir Thomas More*. London: 1891.

Bromiley, Geoffrey W. *Thomas Cranmer, Archbishop and Martyr*. London: 1956.

―――. *Thomas Cranmer, Theologian*. New York: 1956.

Buis, Harry. *Historic Protestantism and Predestination*. Philadelphia: 1958.

Burkill, T. A. *The Evolution of Christian Thought*. Ithaca, New York: 1971.

Burnet, Gilbert. *History of the Reformation of the Church of England*. 2 vols. Edited by Nicholas Pocock. London: 1865.

Bush, Douglas. *The Renaissance and English Humanism*. Toronto: 1939.

―――. "Tudor Humanism and Henry VIII." *University of Totonto Quarterly*. Vol. VII (1938), pp. 162-177.

Butterworth, Charles C. *The English Primers, 1529-1545*. Philadelphia: 1953.

Butterworth, Charles C., and Chester, Allen G. *George Joye*. Philadelphia: 1962.

Campbell, W. E. *Erasmus, Tyndale and More*. London: 1949.

Cargill Thompson, W. D. J. "The Sixteenth Century Editions of A SUPPLICATION UNTO KING HENRY VIII by Robert Barnes, D.D.: a footnote to the history of the royal supremacy." *Transactions of the Cambridge Bibliographical Society*. Vol. III (1960), pp. 133-142.

Carlyle, Edward I. "William Tyndale." *Dictionary of National Biography*. Oxford: 1938.

Caspari, Fritz. *Humanism and the Social Order in Tudor England*. Chicago: 1954.

Chambers, R. W. *Thomas More.* Ann Arbor: 1958.

Chester, Allen G. *Hugh Latimer: Apostle to the English.* Philadelphia: 1954.

———. "Robert Barnes and the Burning of the Books." *Huntington Library Quarterly.* Vol. XIV (May, 1951), pp. 211-221.

Child, Gilbert W. *Church and State Under the Tudors.* London: 1890.

Clebsch, William A. "The Earliest Translations of Luther into English." *Harvard Theological Review.* Vol. 56 (January, 1963), pp. 75-86.

———. *England's Earliest Protestants.* New Haven: 1964.

Constant, G. *The Reformation in England.* 2 vols. Translated by E. I. Watkin. London: 1942.

Cooper, Charles H. *Annals of Cambridge.* 5 vols. Cambridge: 1842-1908.

Cooper, William B. *The Life and Work of William Tyndale.* Toronto: 1924.

Dallmann, William. "King Henry VIII Attacks Luther." *Concordia Theological Monthly.* Vol. 6 (June, 1935), pp. 419-430.

———. *Robert Barnes.* St. Louis: n. d.

———. *William Tyndale.* St. Louis: 1940.

Darby, H. S. *Hugh Latimer.* London: 1953.

———. "Thomas Bilney." *London Quarterly and Holborn Review,* 6th series. Vol. XI (January, 1942), pp. 67-83.

D'Aubigne, J. H. M. *The Reformation in England.* 2 vols. Edited by S. M. Houghton. London: 1963.

Deanesly, Margaret. *The Significance of the Lollard Bible.* London: 1951.

Demaus, Robert. *William Tyndale.* London: 1886.

Devereux, E. J. "Tudor Uses of Erasmus on the Eucharist." *Archiv fuer Reformationsgeschichte.* Vol. 62 (1971), pp. 38-52.

Dickens, A. G. *The English Reformation.* New York: 1964.

———. *Lollards and Protestants in the Dioceses of York.* London: 1959.

———. *Reformation and Society in Sixteenth Century Europe.* New York: 1966.

———. *Thomas Cromwell and the English Reformation.* London: 1959.

Dixon, R. W. *History of the Church of England form the Abolition of the Roman Jurisdiction.* 6 vols. Oxford: 1878-1902.

Doernberg, Erwin. *Henry VIII and Luther.* London: 1961.

Duffield, Gervase, ed. *The Work of William Tyndale.* Philadelphia: 1965.

Dugmore, C. W. *The Mass and the English Reformers.* London: 1958.

Elton, G. R. *England Under the Tudors.* New York: 1955.

———. *Policy and Police: the enforcement of the Reformation in the age of Thomas Cromwell.* Cambridge: 1972.

———. *Reform and Renewal: Thomas Cromwell and the Common Weal.* Cambridge: 1973.

———. "Thomas Cromwell's Decline and Fall." *Cambridge Historical Journal.* Vol. X (1951), pp. 150-185.

Erasmus, Desiderius. *Christian Humanism and the Reformation.* Edited and translated by John C. Olin. New York: 1965.

Fairfield, Leslie P. "John Bale and the Development of Protestant Hagiography." *Journal of Ecclesiastical History.* Vol. 24 (April, 1973), pp. 145-160.

Ferguson, Charles. *Naked to Mine Enemies.* Boston: 1958.

Fisher, H. N. "The Contribution of Robert Barnes to the English Reformation." Unpublished M.A. thesis, University of Birmingham: 1950.

Flesseman-van Leer, E. "The Controversy about Ecclesiology between Thomas More and William Tyndale." *Nederlands Archief voor Kerkgeschiedenis.* Vol. 44 (1960), pp. 65-86.

————. "the Controversy about Scripture and Tradition between Thomas More and William Tyndale." *Nederlandsch Archief voor Kerkgeschiedenis.* Vol. 43 (1959), pp. 143-165.

Fuller, Thomas D. *History of the University of Cambridge.* London: 1655.

————. *History of the Worthies of England.* London: 1662.

Gairdner, James. *The English Church in the Sixteenth Century.* London: 1902.

————. *Lollardy and the Reformation in England.* 4 vols. London: 1908-13.

————. "Robert Barnes, D.D." *Dictonary of National Biography.* Oxford: 1938.

Ganss, H.G. "Sir Thomas More and the Persecution of Heretics." *American Catholic Quarterly.* Vol. 25 (July, 1900), pp. 531-548.

Gee, J.A. "Tindale and the 1533 English ENCHIRIDION." *Publication of the Modern Language Association.* Vol. 49 (1934), pp. 460-471.

Gray, L. F. "William Tyndale: Translator, Scholar and Martyr." *Hibbert Journal.* Vol. 35 (October, 1936), pp. 101-107.

Greenslade, Stanley L. *The English Reformers and the Fathers of the Church.* Oxford: 1960.

————, ed., *The Work of William Tyndale.* London: 1938.

Grisar, Hartmann. *Luther.* 6 vols. Translated by E. M. Lamond. London: 1913-17.

Haas, Steven W. "Simon Fish, William Tyndale and Sir Thomas More's 'Lutheran Conspiracy'." *Journal of Ecclesiastical History.* Vol. 23 (April, 1972), pp. 125-136.

Hagan, Kenneth. "From Testament to Covenant in the early Sixteenth Century." *Sixteenth Century Journal.* Vol. 3 (April, 1972), pp. 1-24.

Hargrave, T. O. "The Doctrine of Predestination in the English Reformation." Unpublished Ph.D. dissertation, Vanderbilt University: 1966.

Headley, John M. "Thomas More and Luther's Revolt." *Archiv fuer Reformationsgeschichte.* Vol. 60 (1969), pp. 145-160.

Heick, Otto W. *A History of Christian Thought.* 2 vols. Philadelphia: 1965.

Hitchcock, James. "More and Tyndale's Controversy over Revelation: a test of the McLuhan hypothesis." *Journal of the American Academy of Religion.* Vol. 39 (December, 1971), pp. 448-466.

Hughes, Philip. *A Popular History of the Reformation.* New York: 1956.

————. *The Reformation in England.* 3 vols. New York: 1951.

Hughes, Philip E. *Theology of the English Reformers.* Grand Rapids: 1965.

Hutchinson, F. E. *Cranmer and the English Reformation.* New York: 1962.

Hyma, Albert. "The Continental Origins of English Humanism." *Huntington Library Quarterly.* Vol. 4 (October, 1940), pp. 1-25.

Jacobs, Henry E. *A Study in Comparative Symbolics: the Lutheran movement in England during the reigns of Henry VIII and Edward VI.* Philadelphia: 1908.

Jones, W. R. D. *The Tudor Commonwealth, 1529-1559.* New York, 1970.

Kennedy, W. P. M. *Studies in Tudor History.* Port Washington, New York: 1971.

Kernan, Gerald. "St. Thomas More, Theologian." *Thought.* Vol. 17 (June, 1942), pp. 281-302.

Knappen, M. M. *Tudor Puritanism.* Chicago: 1939.

————. "William Tindale — First English Puritan." *Church History.* Vol. 5 (April, 1936), pp. 201-215.

Knox, D. B. *The Doctrine of Faith in the Reign of Henry VIII.* London: 1961.

Krodel, G. G. "Luther, Erasmus and Henry VIII." *Archiv fuer Reformationsgeschichte.* Vol. 53 (1962), pp. 60-78.

Lea, Henry C. *History of Sacerdotal Celibacy in the Christian Church.* 4th edition. London: 1932.

Lehmberg, Stanford E. *The Reformation Parliament 1529-1536.* Cambridge: 1970.

Levine, Mortimer, ed. *Tudor England 1485-1603.* Cambridge: 1968.

Lewis, C. S. *English Literature in the Sixteenth Century.* Oxford: 1954.

Loane, Marcus. *Masters of the English Reformation.* London: 1954.

————. *Pioneers of the Reformation in England.* London: 1964.

McAleer, John. "More and his Detractors." *Month,* new series. Vol. 26 (July, 1961), pp. 14-23.

McConica, James K. *English Humanists and Reformation Politics under Henry VIII and Edward VI.* Oxford: 1965.

McDonnell, Kilian. *John Calvin, the Church and the Eucharist.* Princeton: 1967.

Mackie, J. D. *The Earliest Tudors 1485-1558.* Oxford: 1952.

Mackinnon, James. *Luther and the Reformation.* 4 vols. New York: 1925-30.

Maclure, M. *The Paul's Cross Sermons.* Toronto: 1958.

Maitland, S. R. *Essays on the Reformation in England.* London: 1899.

Marius, Richard C. "Thomas More and the Heretics." Unpublished Ph.D. dissertation, Yale University: 1962.

Maynard, Theodore. *Humanist as Hero, the Life of Sir Thomas More.* New York: 1947.

————. *The Life of Thomas Cranmer.* Chicago: 1956.

Bibliography

Meissner, Paul, *England im Zeitalter von Humanismus, Renaissance und Reformation.* Heidelberg: 1952.

Merriman, R. B. *Life and Letters of Thomas Cromwell.* 2 vols. Oxford: 1902.

Meyer, Carl S. "Henry VIII Burns Luther's Books." *Journal of Ecclesiastical History.* Vol. 9 (October, 1958), pp. 173-187.

Miles, Leland. "Persecution and the DIALOGUE OF COMFORT: a fresh look at charges against Thomas More." *Journal of British Studies.* Vol. 5 (November, 1965), pp. 19-30.

Mosse, G. L. "Puritanism Reconsidered." *Archiv fuer Reformationsgeschichte.* Vol. 55 (1964), pp. 37-48.

Mozley, James F. *Coverdale and his Bibles.* London: 1957.

———. *John Foxe and his Book.* London: 1940.

———. "The Supper of the Lord: Tyndale or Joye?" *Moreana.* Vol. 3 (May, 1966), pp. 11-16.

———. *William Tyndale.* New York: 1937.

Muller, James A. *Stephen Gardiner and the Tudor Reaction.* New York: 1926.

Mullinger, James B. *The University of Cambridge.* 3 vols. Cambridge: 1873.

Parker, T. M. *The English Reformation to 1558.* Oxford: 1966.

Pineas, Ranier. "Robert Barnes' Polemical use of History." *Bibliotheque d' Humanisme et Renaissance.* Vol. XXVI (1964), pp. 55-69.

———. *Thomas More and Tudor Polemics.* Bloomington, Indiana: 1968.

———. "Thomas More's Utopia and Protestant Polemics." *Renaissance News.* Vol. 17 (August, 1964), pp. 197-201.

———. "William Tyndale's Influence on John Bale's Polemical Use of History." *Archiv fuer Reformationsgeschichte.* Vol. 53 (1962), pp. 79-96.

———. "William Tyndale's Use of History." *Harvard Theological Review.* Vol. 55 (April, 1962), pp. 121-41.

Plummer, Alfred. *English Church History from the Death of Henry VII to the Death of Archbishop Parker.* Edinburgh: 1905.

Pollard, A. F. *Henry VIII.* New York: 1966.

———. *Thomas Cranmer and the English Reformation.* Hamden, Connecticut: 1905.

———. *Wolsey.* London: 1929.

Pollard, A. W., *et. al.* eds. *Short Title Catalog of Books Printed in England, Scotland and Ireland and of Books Printed Abroad 1475-1640.* London: 1926.

Porter, H. C. *Reformation and Reaction at Tudor Cambridge.* Cambridge: 1958.

Prueser, Friedrich. *England und die Schmalkaldner.* Leipzig: 1929.

Raab, Felix. *The English Face of Machiavelli.* London: 1964.

Read, Conyers, ed. *Bibliography of British History, Tudor Period.* 2nd. edition. Oxford: 1959.

———. *Social and Political Forces in the English Reformation.* Houston: 1953.

Reu, Michael. *Luther and the Scriptures.* Dubuque, Iowa: 1944.

Reynolds, E. E. "More, Coverdale and Cromwell." *Moreana.* Vol. 3 (May, 1966), pp. 77-80.

———. *St. John Fisher.* London: 1955.

———. *St. Thomas More.* Garden City, New York: 1958.

Ridley, Jasper G. *Nicholas Ridley.* London: 1957.

———. *Thomas Cranmer.* Oxford: 1962.

Ross, W. H. *The Beginnings of the English Reformation.* New York: 1957.

Routh, E. M. G. *Sir Thomas More and his Friends.* New York: 1963.

Rupp, E. G. "The Recantation of Thomas Bilney." *London Quarterly and Holborn Review,* 6th series. Vol. XI (April, 1942), pp. 180-186.

———. *Six Makers of English Religion.* London: 1957.

———. *Studies in the Making of the English Protestant Tradition.* Cambridge: 1947.

Russell, Conrad. *The Crisis of Parliaments.* Oxford: 1971.


Saffady, William K. "Heresy and Popular Protestantism in England, 1527-1533." Unpublished Ph.D. dissertation, Wayne State University: 1971.

Scarisbrick, J. J. *Henry VIII.* Berkeley, California: 1968.

Schottenloher, Karl. *Bibliographie zur Deutschen Geschichte im Zeitalter der Glaubensspaltung, 1517-1585.* 7 vols. Stuttgart: 1956.

Smith, H. Maynard. *Henry VIII and the Reformation.* New York: 1948.

———. "The Reformation at Home and Abroad." *Church Quarterly Review.* Vol. 130 (July, 1940), pp. 263-289.

Smith, Lacey Baldwin. "Henry VIII and the Protestant Triumph." *American Historical Review.* Vol. 71 (July, 1966), pp. 1237-1264.

———. *Henry VIII: the Mask of Royalty.* London: 1971.

———. *Tudor Politics and Prelates.* Princeton: 1953.

Smith, Preserved. "Englishmen at Wittenberg in the Sixteenth Century." *English Historical Review.* Vol. 36 (July, 1921), pp. 422-433.

———. "German Opinion of the Divorce of Henry VIII." *English Historical Review.* Vol. 27 (October, 1912), pp. 671-681.

———. *The Life and Letters of Martin Luther.* Boston: 1914.

———. "Luther and Henry VIII." *English Historical Review.* Vol. 25 (October, 1910), pp. 656-669.

———. "Martin Luther and England." *Nation.* Vol. 99 (December 17, 1914), pp. 710-711.

Smithen, Frederick J. *Continental Protestantism and the English Reformation.* London: 1927.

Stacey, John. *John Wyclif and Reform.* Philadelphia: 1964.

Steele, Robert. "Notes on English Books Printed Abroad, 1525-48." *Transactions of the Bibliographical Society.* Vol. XI (1909-11), pp. 189-236.

Sturge, Charles. *Cuthbert Tunstall.* London: 1938.

Surtz, Edward. *The Work and Days of John Fisher.* Cambridge: 1967.

Tjernagel, Neelak, S. "Dr. Robert Barnes and Anglo-Lutheran Relations," 1521-1540." Unpublished Ph.D. dissertation, State, University of Iowa: 1955.

————. *Henry VIII and the Lutherans.* St. Louis: 1965.

Trevelyan, G. M. *England in the Age of Wycliffe.* New York: 1899.

Trinterud, L. J. "A Reappraisal of William Tyndale's Debt to Martin Luther." *Church History.* Vol. 31 (January, 1962), pp. 24-45.

————. "The Origins of Puritanism." *Church History.* Vol. 20 (January, 1951), pp. 37-57.

Walther, D. Wilhelm. *Heinrich VIII von England und Luther.* Leipzig: 1908.

Watkin, E. I. *Roman Catholicism in England from the Reformation to 1950.* London: 1957.

Watson, Philip. *Let God be God.* London: 1947.

Weiss, R. *Humanism in England during the Fifteenth Century.* Oxford: 1941.

Williams, C. H. *William Tyndale.* Stanford, California: 1969.

Williams, Ronald R. *Religion and the English Vernacular.* London 1940.

Wilson, Derek. *A Tudor Tapestry.* Pittsburgh: 1972.

Worsley, Henry. *The Dawn of the English Reformation.* London: 1890.

Yost, John K. "The Christian Humanism of the English Reformers." Unpublished Ph.D. dissertation, Duke University: 1965.

————. "German Protestant Humanism and the Early English Reformation." *Bibliotheque d'Humanisme et Renaissance.* Vol. 32 (1970), pp. 613-625.

————. "Tyndale's use of the Fathers." *Moreana.* Vol. 6 (February, 1969), pp. 5-13.

Zeeveld, W. Gordon. *Foundations of Tudor Policy.* Cambridge: 1948.

# NOTES

## CHAPTER 1

1. Matthew Spinka, ed., *Advocates of Reform,* vol. XIV, *The Library of Christian Classics* (Philadelphia, 1953), pp. 21-31.
2. Margaret Deansley, *The Significance of the Lollard Bible* (London, 1951), pp. 6-9.
3. Margaret Aston, "Lollardy and the Reformation," *History,* new series, XLIX (June, 1964), pp. 149-70.
4. J. S. Brewer, James Gairdner and R. H. Brodie, eds., *Letters and Papers, Foreign and Domestic of the Reign of Henry VIII, 1509-1547,* vol. VI (London, 1882), no. 330 (Hereafter cited as L.P.).
5. Robert Weiss, *Humanism in England During the Fifteenth Century (Oxford, 1941), p. 84 ff.*
6. *The Works of Hugh Latimer,* vol. I, ed., George E. Carrie for the Parker Society (Cambridge, 1845), pp. 334-335.
7. Desiderius Erasmus, "Letter of Jodocus Jonas on Vitrier and Colet," *Christian Humanism and the Reformation,* ed. and trans., John E. Olin (New York, 1961), pp. 184-185.
8. *Ibid.,* p. 178.
9. David B. Knox, *The Doctrine of Faith in the Reign of Henry VIII* (London, 1961), pp. 101-104.
10. *The Acts and Monuments of John Foxe,* ed., George Townsend, vol. 5 (New York, 1965), p. 115 (Hereafter cited as Foxe, *A.M.*).
11. *Ibid.,* vol. 4, p. 230.
12. Erasmus, "The Paraclesis," *Humanism and Reformation,* p. 97.

## CHAPTER 2

1. John Strype, *Ecclesiastical Memorials Relating Chiefly to Religion and the Reformation of it under King Henry VIII,* vol. I (London, 1721), p. 568.
2. Foxe, *A.M.,* vol. V, p. 415.
3. *Ibid.*
4. *Ibid.*
5. John Strype, *Memorials of Archbishop Cranmer,* vol. I (Oxford, 1848), p. 342.
6. *The Works of Hugh Latimer,* vol. I, pp. 334-335.
7. H. Maynard Smith, *Henry VIII and the Reformation* (New York, 1962), p. 254.
8. Lacey Baldwin Smith, *Tudor Prelates and Politics* (Princeton, 1953), p. 35.

Notes

9. Philip Hughes, *The Reformation in England,* vol. I, (New York, 1951).
10. *Letters of Stephen Gardiner,* ed., J. A. Muller (New York, 1953), p. 166.
11. Charles S. Anderson, "Robert Barnes on Luther," *Interpreters of Luther,* ed. Jaroslav Pelikan (Philadelphia, 1968), p. 36.
12. Foxe, *A.M.,* vol. V, p. 416.
13. H. C. Porter, *Reformation and Reaction in Tudor Cambridge* (Cambridge, 1958), p. 48.
14. Foxe, *A. M.,* vol. V, p. 418.
15. *L. P.,* vol. IV, pt. II, no. 4218.
16. Allen G. Chester, "Robert Barnes and the Burning of the Books," *Huntington Library Quarterly,* XIV (May, 1951), 219; Foxe, *A. M.,* vol. V, p. 417; Edward Hall, *The Triumphant Reign of King Henry VIII,* vol. II, ed. Charles Whibley (London, 1904), p. 58.
17. Chester, "Barnes," 221; *L. P.,* vol. XIV, pt. II, nos. 423 and 750.
18. *L. P.,* vol. IV, pt. i, no. 995.
19. Foxe, *A. M.,* vol. V, p. 419.
20. *Ibid.*
21. *Letters of Stephen Gardiner,* pp. 171-172.
22. Robert Barnes, *Vitae Romanorum Pontificium* (Wittenberg, 1536).
23. Foxe, *A. M.,* vol. V, p. 419.
24. Porter, *Tudor Cambridge,* p. 60.
25. Charles S. Anderson, "The Person and Position of Dr. Robert Barnes," (Unpublished Th.D. dissertation, Union Theological Seminary, 1962), p. 19.
26. *Letters of Stephen Gardiner,* p. 165.
27. Robert Barnes, *Sententiae ex Doctoribus Collectae* (Wittenberg, 1530), p. 227.
28. Allen G. Chester, *Hugh Latimer: Apostle to the English* (Philadelphia, 1954), p. 57.
29. Foxe, *A. M.,* vol. p. 419.
30. Erwin Doernberg, *Henry VIII and Luther* (London, 1961), p. 79.
31. Preserved Smith, "Luther and Henry VIII," *English Historical Review,* XXV (October, 1910), 664.
32. *L. P.,* vol. V, no. 533.
33. *Ibid.*
34. *Ibid.*
35. James Gardiner, *Lollardy and the Reformation,* vol. I (London, 1908), p. 307.
36. Neelak S. Tjernagel, *Henry VIII and the Lutherans* (St. Louis, 1965), p. 124.
37. William A. Clebsch, *England's Earliest Protestants* (New Haven, 1964), p. 102.
38. *Ibid.,* p. 287.

39. Cited in E. G. Rupp, *Studies in the Making of the English Protestant Tradition,* (Cambridge, 1966), p. 40.
40. Anderson, "Person and Position," p. 67.
41. H. Maynard Smith, *Henry VIII,* pp. 131-133; *L. P.,* vol. VIII, nos. 1162, 1164, 1170, and 1171.
42. Foxe, *A. M.,* vol. V, pp. 419-420.
43. Gilbert Burnet, *History of the Reformation of the Church of England,* ed., Nicholas Pocock, vol. VI (London, 1865), p. 142, no. XLII; *L. P.,* vol. VIII, nos. 1077, 1078 and 1109.
44. Preserved Smith, "Englishmen at Wittenberg," *English Historical Review,* XXXVI (July, 1921), 424.
45. *L. P.,* vol. X, no. 256; Tjernagel, *Henry VIII,* pp. 163-166.
46. Lacey Baldwin Smith, Henry VIII: *The Mask of Royalty* (London, 1971), p. 123.
47. *L. P.,* vol. VIII, no. 1000.
48. *Ibid.,* no. 771.
49. H. Maynard Smith, *Henry VIII,* p. 129.
50. *L. P.,* vol. X, no. 1034.
51. Chester, *Hugh Latimer,* p. 104.
52. *L. P.,* vol. XIV, pt. ii, no. 107.
53. Rupp, *Protestant Tradition,* p. 43.
54. *L. P.,* vol. XIII, pt. ii, no. 232.
55. *Ibid.,* nos. 204 and 498.
56. Anderson, "Person and Position," p. 119.
57. H. Maynard Smith, *Henry VIII,* p. 170; *L. P.,* vol. XIV, pt. i, nos. 955, 981 and 1273.
58. Foxe, *A. M.,* vol. V, p. 420.
59. Tjernagel, *Henry VIII,* p. 207.
60. Foxe, *A. M.,* vol. V, pp. 262-265.
61. J. A. Muller, *Stephen Gardiner and the Tudor Reaction* (New York, 1926), pp. 79-80.
62. *L. P.,* vol. XIV, pt. i, no. 1278.
63. Martin Luther, *Table Talk,* ed. and trans., T. G. Tappert, vol. 54, *Luther's Works* (Philadelphia, 1967), pp. 361-362.
64. Muller, *Gardiner,* p. 85.
65. J. J. Scarisbrick, *Henry VIII* (Berkeley, 1968), p. 365.
66. Marcus Loane, *Pioneers of the Reformation in England* (London, 1964), p. 79.
67. *L. P.,* vol. XIV, pt. ii, nos. 29, 255 and 400.
68. M. A. S. Hume, ed. and trans., *Chronicles of King Henry VIII of England written in Spanish by an unknown Hand* (London, 1889), p. 194.
69. *L. P.,* vol. XV, no. 259.
70. *Ibid.,* nos. 306 and 485.
71. *Ibid.,* nos. 306 and 334; Tjernagel, *Henry VIII,* pp. 216-217.
72. Foxe, *A. M.,* vol. V, p. 433.

73. Tjernagel, *Henry VIII*, p. 216.
74. *L. P.,* vol. XV, no. 498 (60).
75. *Ibid.,* nos. 495 and 498.
76. Hall, *Henry VIII*, vol. II, p. 309.
77. Foxe, *A. M.,* vol. V, p. 420.
78. Hall, *Henry VIII*, vol. II, p. 309.
79. *Remains of Myles Coverdale,* ed., George Pearson for the Parker Society (Cambridge, 1846), p. 352.
80. Hume, *Chronicle,* p. 196.
81. L. P., vol. XVI, no. 106; Preserved Smith, *The Life and Letters of Martin Luther* (Boston, 1911), p. 198.
82. Philip Melanchthon, *Espistolae, Praefationes, Consilia, Iudicia, Schedae Academicae,* ed., Carolus Gottlieb Bretschneider, vol. III, *Corpus Reformatorum* (Frankfort-am-Main, 1836), no. 1995.
83. W. D. J. Cargill Thompson, "The Sixteenth Century Editions of A SUPPLICATION UNTO KING HENRY THE EIGHTH by Robert Barnes, D.D.: a footnote to the history of the Royal Supremacy," *Transactions of the Cambridge Bibliographical Society,* III (1960), 133-142.
84. Hughes, *Reformation in England,* vol. I, p. 133.
85. Philip Hughes, *A Popular History of the Reformation (Garden City, New York, 1960), p. 152.*
86. Foxe, *A. M.,* vol. V, p. 114.
87. J. F. Mozley, *William Tyndale* (Westport, Connecticut, 1971), p. 5.
88. Foxe, *A. M.,* vol. V, p. 115.
89. William Tyndale, *Expositions and Notes on Sundry Portions of the Holy Scriptures together with the Practice of Prelates,* ed., Henry Walter for the Parker Society (Cambridge, 1849), pp. 206 and 291.
90. Foxe, *A. M.,* vol. V, p. 115.
91. Mozley, *Tyndale,* pp. 17-18.
92. W. E. Campbell, *Erasmus, Tyndale and More* (London, 1949), pp. 100-104.
93. Foxe, *A. M.,* vol. V, p. 115.
94. Mozley, *Tyndale,* p. 24.
95. Foxe, *A. M.,* vol. V, p. 115.
96. Campbell, *Erasmus, Tyndale and More,* p. 103.
97. Foxe, *A. M.,* vol. V, p. 116.
98. William Tyndale, *An Answer to Sir Thomas More's Dialogue,* ed., Henry Walter for the Parker Society (Cambridge, 1850), p. 249.
99. William Tyndale, *Doctrinal Treatises and Introductions to Different Portions of the Holy Scriptures,* ed., Henry Walter for the Parker Society (Cambridge, 1848), p. 394.
100. Foxe, *A. M.,* vol. V, p. 116.
101. *Ibid.,* p. 117.
102. Marcus Loane, *Masters of the English Reformation* (London, 1954), p. 45.

103. Charles Sturge, *Cuthbert Tunstal* (London, 1938), p. 23.
104. Tyndale, *Doctrinal Treatises*, pp. 395-396.
105. J. H. Merle d'Aubigne, *The Reformation in England,* vol. I, ed., S. M. Houghton (London, 1962), p. 193.
106. Tyndale, *Expositions and Notes,* p. 337.
107. Mozley, *Tyndale,* p. 121.
108. *The Works of Hugh Latimer,* vol. I, ed. George E. Carrie for the Parker Society (Cambridge, 1844), pp. 440-441.
109. Foxe, *A. M.,* vol. V, p. 118.
110. *L. P.,* vol. IV, pt. ii, no. 4282.
111. Hughes, *Popular History of the Reformation,* p. 151.
112. Foxe, *A. M.,* vol. V, p. 119.
113. Cited, Mozley, *Tyndale,* p. 52.
114. E. G. Rupp, *Six Makers of English Religion* (London, 1957), p. 18.
115. A. W. Pollard, ed., *Records of the English Bible* (London, 1911), p. 118.
116. Henry Ellis, ed., *Original Letters Illustrative of English History,* vol. III, ii (London, 1824), pp. 74-75.
117. *L. P.,* vol. IV, pt. ii, nos. 4511, 4693 and 5462.
118. Rupp, *Six Makers,* p. 16.
119. Hall, *Henry VIII,* p. 161.
120. *Ibid.;* Foxe, *A. M.,* vol. IV, p. 670.
121. Rupp, *Six Makers,* pp. 20-21.
122. Foxe, *A. M.,* vol. V, p. 119.
123. R. W. Chambers, *Thomas More* (Ann Arbor, 1958), p. 254.
124. John Strype, *Ecclesiastical Memorials relating chiefly to Religion,* vol. I, p. 113.
125. *L. P.,* vol. V, nos. 354, 869, 1554 and 248.
126. *Ibid.,* no. 246.
127. Foxe, *A. M.,* vol. IV, p. 676.
128. *Works of Hugh Latimer,* vol. II, pp. 297-309.
129. Foxe, *A. M.,* vol. IV, pp. 635-655.
130. *L. P.,* vol. V, no. 1554.
131. Foxe, *A. M.,* vol. V, p. 121.
132. *L. P.,* vol. V, nos. 265 and 354.
133. *The Whole Works of W. Tyndale, John Frith and Doct. Barnes* (London, 1573), p. 454.
134. Frith, *Whole Works,* p. i.
135. Tyndale, *Whole Works,* p. 453.
136. Cited, Leland Miles, "Persecution and the Dialogue of Comfort: a fresh look at charges against Thomas More," *Journal of British Studies,* V (November, 1965), p. 28.
137. Foxe, *A. M.,* vol. V, pp. 121-122; Tyndale, *Whole Works,* pp. viii-ix.
138. H. Maynard Smith, *Henry VIII,* p. 331.
139. Foxe, *A. M.,* vol. V, p. 120.
140. *Ibid.,* pp. 122-123; *L. P.,* vol. VIII, no. 1151.

141. *L. P.*, vol. IX, no. 182.

142. *Ibid.*, nos. 498 and 275.

143. Foxe, *A. M.*, vol. V, pp. 124-127.

144. Foxe, *A. M.*, vol. V, p. 127.

145. Hall, *Henry VIII*, p. 267.

146. Foxe, *A. M.*, vol. V, p. 127.

147. Robert Demaus, *William Tyndale* (London, 1886), p. 151.

148. W. B. Cooper, *The Life and Work of William Tyndale* (London, 1925), p. 6.

# CHAPTER 3

1. Otto W. Heick, *A History of Christian Thought*, vol. I (Philadelphia, 1965), p. 257.

2. Introduction, p. 2.

3. Foxe, *A. M.*, vol. III, p. 718.

4. *Ibid.*, p. 720.

5. Kenneth Scott Latourette, *A History of Christianity* (New York, 1953), pp. 456-457.

6. Foxe, *A. M.*, vol. III, p. 245.

7. Stanley L. Greenslade, ed., *The Work of William Tyndale* (London, 1938), p. 29.

8. *Works of Hugh Latimer*, vol. II, p. 389.

9. Charles Wriothesley, *A Chronicle of England During the Reigns of the Tudors*, vol. I, ed., W. D. Hamilton (Westminster, 1875), p. 72.

10. Barnes, *Whole Works*, p. 282.

11. *Ibid.*, p. 283.

12. *Ibid.*, p. 285.

13. *Ibid.*, p. 287.

14. *Ibid.*, p. 285.

15. John Standish, *A lytle treastise against the protestation of Robert Barnes* (London, 1540).

16. *Remains of Myles Coverdale*, p. 414.

17. Barnes, *Whole Works*, p. 288.

18. *Ibid.*, p. 290.

19. Martin Luther, *Career of the Reformer* II, ed. and trans., George W. Forell, vol. 32, *Luther's Works* (Philadelphia, 1958), p. 112.

20. Barnes *Whole Works*, p. 302.

21. Knox, *Doctrine of Faith*, pp. 68 & 80.

22. Barnes, *Whole Works*, p. 209.

23. Jaroslav Pelikan, *Luther the Expositor*, companion volume, *Luther's Works* (Philadelphia, 1959), pp. 48-70; Michael Reu, *Luther and the Scriptures*, (Columbus, 1944). These works give conflicting but equally stimulating views of Luther's doctrine of the Word of God.

24. Barnes, *Whole Works,* p. 289.
25. Neelak S. Tjernagel, ed., *The Reformation Essays of Dr. Robert Barnes* (London, 1963), p. 107.
26. Reu, *Luther and the Scriptures,* p. 27.
27. Luther, *Table Talk,* p. 424.
28. Martin Luther, *Word and Sacrament* I, ed. and trans., E. Theodore Bachmann, vol. 35, *Luther's Works* (Philadelphia, 1960), p. 362.
29. Clebsch, *Earliest Protestants,* pp. 66-67.
30. Heinrich Bornkamm, *Luther and the Old Testament,* trans. E. W. and R. C. Gritsch (Philadelphia, 1969), pp. 87-88.
31. Barnes, *Whole Works,* p. 122.
32. *Ibid.*
33. Theodore G. Tappert, ed. and trans., *The Book of Concord* (Philadelphia, 1959), pp. 141-143.
34. Frith, *Whole Works,* p. 122.
35. Tyndale, *Expositions and Notes,* p. 251.
36. *Ibid.*
37. Tyndale, *Answer to More,* p. 9 (emphasis mine).
38. Tyndale, *Doctrinal Treatises,* p. 103.
39. E. Flessemann-van Leer, "The Controversy about Scripture and Tradition between More and Tyndale." *Nederlandsch Archief voor Kerkgeschiedenis,* 43 (1959), p. 144.
40. Tyndale, *Answer to More,* p. 26.
41. Tyndale, *Doctrinal Treatises,* p. 154.
42. *Ibid.*
43. *Ibid.,* p. 324.
44. Rainer Pineas, *Thomas More and Tudor Polemics* (Bloomington, Indiana, 1968), pp. 102-103.
45. Tyndale, *Answer to More,* p. 130.
46. Barnes, *Whole Works,* p. 307.
47. Tyndale, *Answer to More,* p. 129.
48. Martin Luther, *Lectures on Deuteronomy,* ed. and trans., Jaroslav Pelikan, vol. 9, *Luther's Works* (St. Louis, 1960), p. 188.
49. Tyndale, *Answer to More,* p. 129.
50. *Ibid.,* p. 136.
51. *Ibid.*
52. Tyndale, *Doctrinal Treatises,* p. 394.
53. *Ibid.,* p. 147.
54. Foxe, *A. M.,* vol. V, p. 121.
55. Campbell, Erasmus, *Tyndale and More,* pp. 124-133. Gives helpful summary of More's objections.
56. Chambers, *Thomas More,* p. 252.
57. See chap. 2, note 117.
58. Mozley, *Tyndale,* pp. 345-46. Denies Tyndale wrote prologues to II & III John.

59. Rupp, *Protestant Tradition*, p. 501 (emphasis mine).
60. Mozley, *Tyndale*, p. 285.
61. Tyndale, *Doctrinal Treatises*, p. 525.
62. Demaus, *Tyndale*, p. 241.
63. Tyndale, *Expositions and Notes*, p. 142.
64. *Ibid.*, p. 196.
65. Tyndale, *Doctrinal Treatises*, p. 167.
66. Martin Luther, *Lectures on Galatians* 1535, ed. and trans. Jaroslav Pelikan, vol. 26, *Luther's Works* (St. Louis, 1963), pp. 208-209.
67. Tyndale, *Doctrinal Treatises*, pp. 8-11.
68. L. J. Trinterud, "A Reappraisal of William Tyndale's Debt to Martin Luther," *Church History*, 31 (January 1962), 24-45. Correctly indicates that Tyndale eventually adopted a Calvinist position on the role of the law in the Christian life but exaggerates the cleavage between Calvin and Luther.
69. Tyndale, *Whole Works*, p. 142.
70. *Ibid.*, p. 172.
71. Barnes, *Whole Works*, p. 301.
72. Tyndale, *Whole Works*, p. 172.
73. Tyndale, *Doctrinal Treatises*, p. 304.
74. *Ibid.*, p. 307.
75. *Ibid.*, p. 305.
76. *Ibid.*, p. 411.
77. *Ibid.*, p. 215.
78. Tyndale, *Answer to More*, p. 139.
79. Flessemann van-Leer, "Controversy about Scripture and Tradition," p. 154.
80. *Ibid.*, p. 161.
81. Tyndale, *Doctrinal Treatises*, p. 107.
82. Tyndale, *Expositions and Notes*, p. 100.
83. Rupp, *Six Makers*, p. 13.

## Chapter 4

1. Luther, *Career of the Reformer* IV, p. 201.
2. See chap. 2, note 48.
3. Martin Luther, *Church and Ministry* II, ed. and trans., Conrad Bergendoff, vol. 40, *Luther's Works* (Philadelphia, 1958), p. 86-87.
4. Martin Luther, *Devotional Writings* II, ed. and trans., Gustav K. Wiencke, vol. 43, *Luther's Works* (Philadelphia, 1968), p. 43.
5. Barnes, *Whole Works*, pp. 339-355.
6. *Ibid.*, p. 339.
7. *Ibid.*, p. 353.
8. *Ibid.*, p. 342.
9. *Ibid.*, p. 343.
10. *Ibid.*, p. 344.
11. *Ibid.*, p. 345-346.

12. *Ibid.*, p. 346.
13. *Ibid.*
14. Tyndale, *Answer to More,* pp. 56-59.
15. *Ibid.*, p. 60.
16. *Ibid.*, p. 62.
17. *Ibid.*, p. 59.
18. *Ibid.*, p. 62.
19. Martin Luther, *Word and Sacrament* II, ed. and trans., Abdel Ross Wentz, vol. 36, *Luther's Works* (Philadelphia, 1959), p. 87.
20. Martin Luther, *Church, and Ministry* III, ed. and trans., Eric W. Gritsch, vol. 41, *Luther's Works* (Philadelphia, 1966), p. 204.
21. Barnes, *Whole Works,* p. 347.
22. *Ibid.*, p. 349.
23. *Ibid.*, p. 351.
24. Tyndale, *Answer to More,* pp. 95-96.
25. *Ibid.*, p. 116.
26. *Ibid.*, p. 131.
27. *Ibid.*, p. 279.
28. Tyndale, *Doctrinal Treatises,* p. 271.
29. Tyndale, *Expositions and Notes,* p. 164.
30. Barnes, *Whole Works,* p. 301.
31. Luther, *Word and Sacrament* II, p. 298.
32. Cited, Barnes, *Whole Works,* p. 350.
33. Martin Luther, *Lectures on Romans,* ed. and trans., Wilhelm Pauck, vol. XV, *Library of Christian Classics* (Philadelphia, 1961), pp. 23-26.
34. Martin Luther, *Sermons on the Gospel of John,* ed and trans., Jaroslav Pelikan, vol 22, *Luther's Works* (St. Louis, 1957), pp. 150-151.
35. Luther, *Lectures on Galatians* 1535, pp. 399-400.
36. Philip S. Watson, *Let God be God* (London, 1947), pp. 73-101. Contains an incisive discussion of Luther's concept of revelation.
37. Tyndale, *Doctrinal Treatises,* p. 160.
38. Conyers Read, *The Tudors* (New York, 1936), p. 46.
39. Martin Luther, *Lectures on Genesis,* ed. and trans., Jaroslav Pelikan, vol. 1, *Luther's Works* (St. Louis, 1958), p. 57.
40. *Ibid.*, p. 63.
41. Heick, *History of Christian Thought,* vol. I, p. 198.
42. Bengt Haegglund, *History of Theology* (St. Louis, 1968), pp. 137-138.
43. Harry J. McSorley, *Luther: Right or Wrong?* (Minneapolis, 1969), pp. 215-224. A modern Catholic reappraisal of Luther's doctrine of the will.
44. Barnes, *Whole Works,* pp. 266-282.
45. *Ibid.*, p. 266.
46. *The Reformation Essays of Dr. Robert Barnes,* p. 64.

47. Barnes, *Whole Works*, p. 268.
48. *Ibid.*, p. 270.
49. *Ibid.*, p. 271.
50. Heick, *History of Christian Thought*, vol. I, p. 289.
51. Barnes, *Whole Works*, p. 273.
52. *Ibid.*, p. 276.
53. *Ibid.*, p. 281.
54. *Ibid.*
55. Martin Luther, *The Bondage of the Will*, trans., J. I. Packer and O. R. Johnston (Westwood, N.J., 1957).
56. Tyndale, *Answer to More*, p. 209.
57. Tyndale, *Doctrinal Treatises*, p. 489.
58. *Ibid.*, p. 491.
59. Tyndale, *Expositions and Notes*, p. 199.
60. Tyndale, *Answers to More*, p. 204.
61. Tyndale, *Doctrinal Treatises*, p. 485.
62. Luther, *Career of the Reformer* IV, p. 111.
63. Tyndale, *Answer to More*, p. 192.
64. Tyndale, *Expositions and Notes*, p. 199.
65. Tyndale, *Doctrinal Treatises*, p. 183.
66. Tyndale, *Answer to More*, p. 140.
67. *Ibid.*, p. 175.
68. Luther, *Bondage of the Will*, p. 209.

## Chapter 5

1. Harry Buis, *Historic Protestantism and Predestination* (Philadelphia, 1958). Contains discussions on each leading Protestant thinker.
2. Barnes, *Whole Works*, pp. 278-279.
3. *Ibid.*, p. 274.
4. *Reformation Essays of Dr. Robert Barnes*, p. 72.
5. Barnes, *Whole Works*, p. 276.
6. cf. Luther, *Bondage of the Will*, pp. 170-171.
7. Luther, *Lectures on Romans*, p. 247.
8. Barnes, *Whole Works*, p. 235.
9. Tyndale, *Doctrinal Treatises*, p. 113.
10. *Ibid.*, p. 505.
11. *Ibid.*, p. 64.
12. *Ibid.*, p. 65.
13. *Ibid.*, p. 23.
14. Tyndale, *Answer to More*, p. 35.
15. *Ibid.*, p. 36.
16. Tyndale, *Doctrinal Treatises*, p. 19.
17. Martin Luther, *Small Catechism* (Philadelphia, 1874), p. 12.
18. Heick, *History of Christian Thought*, vol. I, pp. 275-276.

19. *Reformation Essays of Dr. Robert Barnes,* pp. 72-73.
20. Tyndale, *Answer to More,* p. 149.
21. Tyndale, *Expositions and Notes,* p. 157.
22. *Ibid.,* p. 167.
23. Barnes, *Whole Works,* p. 229.
24. Tappert, *Book of Concord,* p. 292.
25. Barnes, *Whole Works,* p. 235.
26. Tyndale, *Answer to More,* p. 169.
27. Luther, *Word and Sacrament* I, pp. 22 & 370.
28. Tyndale, *Doctrinal Treatises,* p. 13.
29. Heick, *History of Christian Thought,* vol. I, p. 289.
30. Luther, *Career of the Reformer* IV, p. 151ff.
31. *Ibid.,* p. 151.
32. Greenslade, *Work of William Tindale,* p. 39.
33. Barnes, *Whole Works,* p. 235.
34. Tyndale, *Expositions and Notes,* p. 103.
35. Barnes, *Whole Works,* p. 235.
36. *Ibid.* (emphasis mine).
37. Greenslade, *Work of William Tindale,* p. 27.
38. Tyndale, *Doctrinal Treatises,* p. 224.
39. *Ibid.,* p. 471.
40. Tyndale, *Answer to More,* pp. 114 & 127.
41. *Ibid.,* pp. 22-23.
42. Barnes, *Whole Works,* p. 226.
43. Tyndale, *Expositions and Notes,* p. 14.
44. Augustine, *Later Works,* ed. and trans., John Burnaby, vol. VIII, *Library of Christian Classics* (Philadelphia, 1955), pp. 182-250.
45. Luther, *Career of the Reformer* IV, p. 111.
46. Tyndale, *Doctrinal Treatises,* pp. 125-126.
47. Barnes, *Whole Works,* p. 236.
48. Tyndale, *Doctrinal Treatises,* pp. 20-21.
49. Tyndale, *Expositions and Notes,* p. 13.
50. *Ibid.,* p. 35.
51. C. S. Lewis, *English Literature in the Sixteenth Century* (Oxford, 1954), p. 188.
52. Barnes, *Whole Works,* p. 236.
53. *Ibid.*
54. Tyndale, *Doctrinal Treatises,* p. 526.
55. Tyndale, *Answer to More,* pp. 8 & 200-204.
56. *Reformations Essays of Dr. Robert Barnes,* p. 33.
57. Tyndale, *Doctrinal Treatises,* pp. 23-24.
58. *Ibid.,* p. 100.
59. *Ibid.,* p. 102.
60. Martin Luther, *Christian in Society* II, ed. and trans., Walther I. Brandt, vol. 45, *Luther's Works* (Philadelphia, 1962), pp. 161-194.
61. Tyndale, *Doctrinal Treatises,* p. 82.

Notes

62. *Ibid.*
63. Barnes, *Whole Works,* p. 345.
64. *Ibid.,* pp. 207-208.
65. Tyndale, *Doctrinal Treatises,* p. 56.
66. Martin Luther, *Lectures on Galatians* 1535, ed. and trans., Jaroslav Pelican, vol. 27, *Luther's Works* (St. Louis, 1964), p. 230.
67. Luther, *Career of the Reformer* II, p. 239.
68. Tyndale, *Expositions and Notes,* p. 9.
69. *Ibid.,* p. 76.
70. *Ibid.,* p. 10.
71. cf. Rupp, *Protestant Tradition;* Mozley, *Tyndale: Demaus, Tyndale;* Tjernagel, *Henry VIII;* Henry E. Jacobs, *The Lutheran Movement in England* (Philadelphia, 1908).
72. cf. Clebsch, *Earliest Protestants;* L. J. Trinterud, "A Reappraisal of William Tyndale's Debt to Luther," *Church History,* 31 (March, 1962), pp. 24-25; John K. Yost, "The Christian Humanism of the English Reformers," unpublished Ph. D. dissertation, Duke University, 1965; "German Protestant Humanism and the Early English Reformation," *Bibliotheque d'Humanisme et Renaissance,* 32 (1970), pp. 613-625.
73. Paul Althaus, *The Theology of Martin Luther,* trans., Robert C. Schultz (Philadelphia, 1966), pp. 266-273. Gives a penetrating analysis of Luther on the law and the Christian.
74. Luther, *Bondage of the Will,* p. 180.
75. Luther, *Church and Ministry* II, p. 98.
76. Luther, *Lectures on Galatians* 1535, vol. 27, *Luther's Works,* p. 224.
77. Clebsch, *Earliest Protestants,* p. 174.
78. *Ibid.,* p. 155.
79. See chap. 3, "Robert Basrnes on Authority."
80. Clebsch, *Earliest Protestants,* p. 174.
81. *Ibid.,* p. 183.
82. *Ibid.,* p. 191.
83. Trinterud, "Reappraisal of Tyndale's Debt to Luther," p. 27ff.
84. Yost, "Christian Humanism of the English Reformers," pp. 79-80.
85. Luther, *Career of the Reformer* IV, p. 109 ff.
86. Tyndale, *Expositions and Notes,* pp. 147, 150, 155, 157, 163, etc.
87. *Ibid.,* p. 166.
88. Luther, *Career of the Reformer* II, p. 239.
89. Clebsch, *Earliest Protestants,* p. 172.
90. Sir Thomas More, *The Confutation of Tyndale's Answer,* fascile IV, *The Complete Works of St. Thomas More, Kt.,* ed., Frank Sullivan (Los Angeles, 1957).
91. Mozley, *Tyndale,* pp. 233-234.
92. L. J. Trinterud, "The Origins of Puritanism," *Church History,* 20 (March, 1951), 37-57.
93. See chap. 3, note 67.

94. Cited, Foxe, *A. M.,* vol. V, pp. 132-133.
95. Barnes, *Whole Works,* pp. 272 & 288.

## Chapter 6

1. See chap. 3, "The Nature of the Problem."
2. T. A. Burkill, *The Evolution of Christian Thought* (Ithaca, New 1971), pp. 197-198.
3. Luther, *Church and Ministry* II, p. 37.
4. Martin Luther, *Word and Sacrament* III, ed. and trans., Robert Fischer, vol. 37, *Luther's Works* (Philadelphia, 1961), p. 368.
5. Luther, *Church and Ministry* III, pp. 9-178.
6. Luther, *Word and Sacrament* III, p. 367.
7. Luther, *Word and Sacrament* I, pp. 410-411.
8. Burkill, *Evolution of Christian Thought,* p. 197.
9. cf. Luther, *Church and Ministry* II, pp. 61-72 & 73-224.
10. *Ibid.,* p. 21.
11. *Ibid.,* pp. 21-32.
12. Luther, *Word and Sacrament* II, p. 88.
13. *Ibid.,* pp. 85-89.
14. Barnes, *Whole Works,* pp. 242-256.
15. *Ibid.,* p. 250.
16. *Ibid.,* p. 244.
17. *Ibid.,* p. 243.
18. *Ibid.,* p. 244.
19. *Ibid.,* pp. 252-256.
20. *Ibid.,* p. 255.
21. *Ibid.,* p. 251.
22. *Ibid.,* p. 244.
23. Norman H. Fischer, "The Contribution of Robert Barnes to the English Reformation," (unpublished M.A. thesis, University of Birmingham, 1950), pp. 204-206.
24. Barnes, *Whole Works,* p. 262.
25. *Reformation Essays of Dr. Robert Barnes,* p. 39.
26. Barnes, *Whole Works,* p. 286.
27. *Ibid.,* pp. 257-266.
28. *Ibid.,* pp. 260-261.
29. *Ibid.,* p. 261.
30. *Ibid.,* pp. 259-260.
31. *Ibid.,* p. 262.
32. *Ibid.,* p. 265.
33. cf. note 5.
34. cf. *Reformation Essays of Dr. Robert Barnes,* p. 52 note.
35. See chap. 5, note 95.
36. See chap. 2, note 22.
37. Clebsch, *Earliest Protestants,* p. 73.

38. Barnes, *Vitae Romanorum Pontificum,* pp. 1-2, trans., M. M. Knappen, *Tudor Puritanism* (Chicago, 1929), p. 64.
39. *Ibid.*
40. Luther, *Table Talk,* pp. 333 & 397.
41. Tyndale, *Doctrinal Treatises,* p. 319.
42. Tyndale, *Expositions and Notes,* p. 281.
43. *Ibid.*
44. Tyndale, *Answer to More,* p. 13.
45. *Ibid.,* p. 107.
46. *Ibid.,* pp. 39-40.
47. *Ibid.,* p. 45.
48. *Ibid.,* p. 32; cf. E. Flessman van Leer, "The Controversy about Ecclesiology between Thomas More and William Tyndale," *Nederlandsch Archief voor Kerkgeschiedenis,* 44 (1960), 65-86.
49. Greenslade, *Work of William Tyndale,* pp. 30-31.
50. Tyndale, *Whole Works,* p. 291.
51. *Ibid.*
52. Tyndale, *Answer to More,* p. 142.
53. cf. Tyndale, *Doctrinal Treatises,* pp. 255-256, 506, & 527.
54. *Ibid.,* p. 256.
55. Tyndale, *Expositions and Notes,* p. 36.
56. Tyndale, *Doctrinal Treatises,* p. 256.
57. Tyndale, *Answer to More,* p. 17.
58. Tyndale, *Expositions and Notes,* pp. 181-182.
59. *Ibid.,* p. 242.
60. Demaus, *Tyndale,* p. 209.
61. Tyndale, *Doctrinal Treatises,* pp. 236 & 271.
62. Tyndale, *Expositions and Notes,* p. 160.
63. *Ibid.,* p. 12.
64. Tyndale, *Doctrinal Treatises,* p. 272.
65. *Ibid.,* p. 206.
66. Mozley, *Tyndale,* p. 218.
67. Barnes, *Whole Works,* p. 256.
68. Heick, *History of Christian Thought,* vol. I, pp. 290-291.
69. *Ibid.,* p. 290.
70. A. G. Dickens, *Reformation and Society in Sixteenth Century Europe* (New York, 1966), p. 60.
71. Luther, *Word and Sacrament* II, pp. 5-126.
72. Luther, *Church and Ministry* II, pp. 21-23.
73. Luther, *Career of the Reformer* II, p. 15.
74. Luther, *Word and Sacrament* II, p. 67.
75. Luther, *Career of the Reformer* II, p. 15.
76. Luther, *Small Catechism,* pp. 17-18.
77. *Ibid.,* p. 18.
78. Luther, *Word and Sacrament* I, p. 33.

79. Luther, *Church and Ministry* II, p. 239ff.
80. Tappert, *Book of Concord*, pp. 443-444.
81. *Ibid.*, p. 443.
82. Luther, *Small Catechism*, pp. 19-20.
83. Luther, *Word and Sacrament* II, pp. 34-35.
84. Luther, *Word and Sacrament* III, p. 317.
85. Luther, *Small Catechism*, p. 20.
86. Luther, *Word and Sacrament* I, p. 91.
87. Luther, *Word and Sacrament* III, p. 238.
88. Foxe, *A.M.*, vol. V, p. 434.
89. Cited from *Bekantnus dess Glaubens die Doctor Robert Barnes* (Wittenberg, c. 1540); Anderson, "Person and Position," p. 233.
90. Barnes, *Whole Works*, pp. 346-358.
91. *The Catechism of the Council Trent*, trans., J. Donovan (New York, 1829), pp. 171-172.
92. Luther, *Word and Sacrament* II, pp. 231-267.
93. Barnes, *Whole Works*, p. 303.
94. *Ibid.*, pp. 301-303.
95. *Ibid.*, p. 303.
96. *Ibid.*, p. 306.
97. *Ibid.*, p. 308.
98. Knox, *Doctrine of Faith*, p. 80, note 1., would be well advised to exercise more caution before making the unqualified statement that "Barnes was the only English reformer who accepted Luther's doctrine of consubstantiation."
99. See chap. 2, note 48.
100. Foxe, *A.M.*, vol. V, pp. 225-235.
101. *Remains of Myles Coverdale*, p. 417.
102. Tjernagel, *Henry VIII*, pp. 228-229.
103. Foxe, *A.M.*, vol. V, pp. 440-442; Hall, *Henry VIII*, vol. II, p. 311.
104. James Gairdner, *The English Church in the Sixteenth Century* (London, 1902), p. 220.
105. Foxe, *A.M.*, vol. V, p. 10.
106. Henry C. Lea, *History of Sacerdotal Celibacy in the Christian Church*, 4th ed., (London, 1932), pp. 367-368.
107. Barnes, *Whole Works*, p. 310.
108. *Ibid.*, p. 310.
109. *Ibid.*, p. 312.
110. *Ibid.*, p. 313.
111. *Ibid.*, p. 317.
112. *Ibid.*, p. 319.
113. Lea, *Sacerdotal Celibacy*, pp. 56 & 79.
114. Barnes, *Whole Works*, pp. 327-328.
115. Luther, *Christian in Society* II, pp. 11-49.
116. Tyndale, *Doctrinal Treatises*, pp. 252-253 ff.
117. *Ibid.*, p. 369.

118. *Ibid.,* p. 283.
119. Tyndale, *Answer to More,* p. 27.
120. Tyndale, *Doctrinal Treatises,* p. 253.
121. *Ibid.,* pp. 26 & 261.
122. See chap. 6, "Martin Luther on the Sacraments."
123. Tyndale, *Doctrinal Treatises,* pp. 350-351.
124. *Ibid.,* p. 350.
125. *Ibid.,* p. 351.
126. *Ibid.,* p. 350.
127. Tyndale, *Expositions and Notes,* p. 90.
128. Tyndale, *Doctrinal Treatises,* pp. 359-362.
129. Tyndale, *Answer to More,* p. 65.
130. Tyndale, *Doctrinal Treatises,* p. 424.
131. *Ibid.,* pp. 366-369.
132. *Ibid.,* p. 369.
133. *Ibid.,* p. 372.
134. *Ibid.,* p. 360.
135. Tyndale, *Answer to More,* p. 177.
136. cf. John Calvin, *Institutes of the Christian Religion,* 2 vols., ed. and trans., John Allen (Philadelphia, 1936), IV, p. 17; John Calvin, *Instruction in Faith* (1537), ed. and trans., Paul T. Fuhrmann (Philadelphia, 1949), pp. 69-71; John K. Yost, "Tyndale's Use of the Fathers," *Moreana,* vol. 6 (February, 1969), pp. 5-13; L. J. Trinterud, "The Origins of Puritanism," *Church History,* vol. 20 (March, 1951), p. 39.
137. Foxe, *A.M.,* vol. V, p. 133.
138. Edward Carlyle is surely in error in stating that Tyndale adopted a Zwinglian view of the Eucharist "through the persuasions of Robert Barnes." cf. "William Tyndale," *Dictionary of National Biography,* vol. 19, eds. Sir Leslie Stephan and Sir. Sidney Lee (Oxford, 1938), p. 1352.
139. Tyndale, *Doctrinal Treatises,* pp. 384-385.
140. *Ibid.,* p. 254.
141. Tyndale, *Expositions and Notes,* p. 295.
142. Tyndale, *Doctrinal Treatises,* p. 230.
143. *Ibid.,* p. 439.
144. Demaus, *Tyndale,* p. 250.
145. Tyndale, *Expositions and Notes,* p. 319 ff.
146. Ulrich Zwingli, "Of Baptism," *Zwingli and Bullinger,* ed. and trans., G. W. Bromiley, vol. XXIV, *Library of Christian Classics* (Philadelphia, 1953), pp. 119-175.

## Chapter 7

1. Demaus, *Tyndale,* p. 485.

2. Luther, *Christian in Society* II, p. 83; cf. Heinrich Bornkamm, *Luther's Doctrine of the Two Kingdoms*, trans., K. H. Hertz (Philadelphia, 1966).

3. Luther, *Christian in Society* II, p. 85.

4. *Ibid.*, p. 87.

5. *Ibid.*, p. 90.

6. *Ibid.*, p. 96.

7. *Ibid.*, p. 100.

8. *Ibid.*, p. 111.

9. *Ibid.*, pp. 111-112.

10. *Ibid.*, p. 117.

11. William K. Saffaday, "Heresy and Popular Protestantism in England, 1527-1533," (unpublished Ph.D. dissertation, Wayne State University, 1971), p. 115.

12. Barnes, *Whole Works*, p. 183 ff; Rainer Pineas, "Robert Barnes' Polemical Use of History," *Bibliotheque d'Humanisme et Renaissance*, vol. XXVI (February, 1964), pp. 55-69. Gives an incisive analysis of Barnes as polemicist.

13. Barnes, *Whole Works*, p. 202.

14. *Ibid.*, pp. 185-186.

15. *Ibid.*, p. 185.

16. *Ibid.*, pp. 201-202.

17. *Ibid.*, pp. 186-187.

18. *Ibid.*, p. 189.

19. cf. Luther, *Christian in Society* II, pp. 118-129.

20. Barnes, *Whole Works*, p. 191.

21. *Ibid.*, pp. 195-196.

22. Clebsch, *Earliest Protestants*, pp. 62-63.

23. *Ibid.*, p. 200.

24. Barnes, *Whole Works*, p. 205.

25. *Ibid.*, pp. 292-297.

26. Apparently Fisher was unaware that the essay, "Men's constitutions . . ." was omitted from the final edition of the *Supplication*. He portrays Barnes as an unyielding adherent to the two kingdoms concept. cf. "The Contribution of Robert Barnes," pp. 166-175.

27. Barnes, *Whole Works*, pp. 292-293.

28. *Remains of Myles Coverdale*, pp. 436-438; Foxe, *A.M.*, vol. V, pp. 435-436.

29. Tyndale, *Expositions and Notes*, p. 60.

30. *Ibid.*, p. 62.

31. *Ibid.*, p. 63.

32. *Ibid.*, p. 53.

33. *Ibid.*, p. 65.

34. *Ibid.*, p. 66.

35. *Ibid.*, pp. 36 & 86.

36. Tyndale, *Doctrinal Treatises*, p. 177.
37. Tyndale, *Expositions and Notes*, p. 53.
38. Foxe, *A.M.*, vol. V, p. 119.
39. Campbell, *Erasmus, Tyndale and More*, p. 112.
40. A. F. Pollard, *Wolsey* (London, 1929), p. 359.
41. Mozley, *Tyndale*, pp. 143-144.
42. Luther, *Christian in Society* II, pp. 75-129.
43. cf. Steven Haas, "Simon Fish, William Tyndale, and Sir Thomas More's 'Lutheran Conspiracy'," *Journal of Ecclesiastical History 23 (April, 1972), 125-136.*
44. Tyndale, *Doctrinal Treatises*, p. 163.
45. *Ibid.*, p. 173.
46. *Ibid.*, pp. 175-180 & 194.
47. *Ibid.*, pp. 185-189.
48. *Ibid.*, pp. 206-207; *Expositions and Notes*, p. 247.
49. Tyndale, *Doctrinal Treatises*, p. 282.
50. *Ibid.*, p. 338.
51. *Ibid.*, pp. 328 & 338-39.
52. *Ibid.*, p. 240.
53. Ibid., pp. 338-339; *Expositions and Notes*, p. 19.
54. Ranier Pineas, "William Tyndale's Influence on John Bale's Polemical Use of History," *Archiv fuer Reformationsgeschichte*, 53 (1962), 83. cf. Barnes, *Whole Works*, pp. 194 & 201-202.
55. Tyndale, *Expositions and Notes*, pp. 244-245.
56. Demaus, *Tyndale*, p. 195.
57. cf. Ranier Pineas, "William Tyndale's Use of History," *Harvard Theological Review*, vol. 55 (April, 1962), pp. 121-141. Examines Tyndale's conspiratorial view of history.
58. The present writer must disagree with Professor Knappen when he charges Tyndale with failure to abide by his own doctrine of obedience by fleeing England and then flooding his homeland with prohibited books. It seems that Knappen understands Tyndale to teach absolute obedience while practicing a kind of "Puritan insubordination." This is surely incorrect. Tyndale was exactly true to his own principles when he refused obedience where the royal will prohibited the furtherance of the Gospel. Cf. M. M. Knappen, *Tudor Puritanism* (Chicago, 1939), p. 65.
59. Hughes, *Theology of the English Reformers*, pp. 246-247.
60. Tyndale, *Doctrinal Treatises*, p. 202; cf. *Expositions and Notes*, p. 35.
61. Martin Luther, *Letters* II, ed. and trans., Gottfried G. Krodel, vol. 49, *Luther's Works* (Philadelphia, 1972), pp. 429-433.

## Chapter 8

1. cf. Tjernagel, *Henry VIII*, pp. 250-254.

# INDEX

Index

# VITA

Dr. James Edward McGoldrick is a professor of history at Cedarville College in Cedarville, Ohio, where he teaches European History, with specialization in the fields of British History, Renaissance-Reformation, and the History of Christian Thought.

Before joining the Cedarville faculty in 1973, the author taught at John Brown University in Siloam Springs, Arkansas, and at West Virginia University, where he also earned his Ph.D.

Professor McGoldrick currently holds membership in the American Society of Church History, Conference on Faith and History, Sixteenth Century Studies Conference, and the American Society for Reformation Research. His published articles have appeared in *Christian Economics, Modern Age,* the *University of Dayton Review,* and *Fides et Historica.*